Karzai

Hamid Karzai, president of Afghanistan.

Karzai

The Failing American Intervention
and the Struggle for Afghanistan

NICK B. MILLS

John Wiley & Sons, Inc.

This book is dedicated to my daughters, Nicole and Sara

Published by John Wiley & Sons, Inc., Hoboken, New Jersey
Published simultaneously in Canada

Design and composition by Navta Associates, Inc.

For general information about our other products and services, please contact our Customer Care Department within the United States at (800) 762-2974, outside the United States at (317) 572-3993 or fax (317) 572-4002.

Wiley also publishes its books in a variety of electronic formats. Some content that appears in print may not be available in electronic books. For more information about Wiley products, visit our web site at www.wiley.com.

Library of Congress Cataloging-in-Publication Data:
Mills, Nick, date.
  Karzai : the failing American intervention and the struggle for Afghanistan / Nick B. Mills.
      p. cm.
  Includes index.
  ISBN 978-0-470-13400-9 (cloth)
  1. Afghanistan—History—Soviet occupation, 1979–1989. 2. Afghanistan—History—1989–2001. 3. Afghanistan—History—2001– 4. Karzai, Hamid, 1957– I. Title.
  DS371.4.M56 2007
  958.104—dc22
                                                                                  2007026599
Printed in the United States of America

10 9 8 7 6 5 4 3 2 1

Contents

Preface   vii

Acknowledgments   xiii

A Brief History of Afghanistan   1

Introduction   11

1   Hamid Karzai   21

2   The Beginning of Jihad   43

3   Defeating a Superpower   59

4   Losing the Peace: As the World Withdraws   75

5   The Rise of the Taliban   95

6   September 11, 2001: The War on Terror Begins
     in Afghanistan   143

7   The Fall of the Taliban: A New Beginning for
     Afghanistan   161

8   Building a New Afghanistan   183

9   Progress, Promise, and Problems: The Road Ahead   207

Epilogue   225

Index   235

Illustrations follow page 112

Preface

I first met Hamid Karzai in 1987 in Peshawar, Pakistan, as I was recruiting Afghan trainees for the Afghan Media Project, for which Boston University's College of Communication had hired me as field director. The media project led to the founding of the Afghan Media Resource Center (AMRC), a full-service Afghan news agency. Karzai was my contact at the Afghan National Liberation Front (ANLF), one of the seven major Afghan resistance parties engaged in the struggle to drive the Soviet Union out of Afghanistan. Some of the parties, particularly the fundamentalist groups that preached a hatred of the West, were difficult to deal with and reluctant to participate in the project, which would train Afghans in journalism. In that context, the ANLF was refreshingly friendly, all the more so because Hamid Karzai was warm and welcoming, and he spoke English fluently. I was impressed. Karzai and I met once or twice officially, and a few times in the Peshawar social scene, where Westerners, Afghans, and Pakistanis mingled. I left Peshawar at the end of August 1988 to take up a teaching position at Boston University and did not see Hamid Karzai again for sixteen years. By then, he was president of the interim government of Afghanistan.

In 2004, I had the opportunity to spend the summer in Kabul working as an adviser and journalism trainer in the Office of the Spokesperson for the President (OSP), Karzai's press office. Finally seeing Kabul, after all that I had heard about it from my Afghan friends, was a thrill. Entering the Arg Palace on a six-day-a-week basis to work for Jawed Ludin, the president's spokesman, was an exciting privilege. Some of the men we had trained in Peshawar were now in Kabul, and two were working in the palace: Hamed Elmi was deputy spokesman, and Abdul Saboor was the president's official photographer. Another AMRC graduate, Ekram Shinwari, was the Voice of America's Pashto reporter in Kabul.

I did not see much of Karzai that summer. Once he came over from his office in the Gulkhana to say hello to the people in the OSP next door, and we chatted briefly about Peshawar days, and we would nod hello at news conferences held under the towering old trees in the palace garden. When I left at the end of the summer, Deputy Spokesman Elmi handed me a hefty keepsake, a metal box covered with polished inlaid lapis lazuli and agate. Inside was a small card that read, "A Gift From the President of Afghanistan, His Excellency Hamid Karzai." No signature.

In early 2005 a Boston University vice president, Joseph Mercurio, asked me to invite President Karzai to be Boston University's commencement speaker. I called Jawed Ludin, who was now the president's chief of staff. He was doubtful, but he said, after checking his calendar, "The date is open. Let me ask the president." A day later, Ludin called my cell phone and said, "The president accepts. He would like to do it." I was elated.

The night before commencement, Karzai was welcomed

to a cold and rainy Boston by Massachusetts governor Mitt Romney, who had arranged a ceremony complete with an honor guard and a colonial fife-and-drum unit in an airport hangar. The following day the rain held off and an audience of twenty-five thousand graduates, parents, family, and friends gathered at BU's Nickerson Field gave Karzai a hero's welcome. He reminded the students of the interconnectedness of the world and the perils of ignoring a small, poor nation like Afghanistan, perils that were realized in the horror of 9/11.

Before Karzai's visit to Boston I had met literary agent Helen Rees, whose authors include former General Electric CEO Jack Welch and his wife, Suzie, and noted attorney Alan Dershowitz. Helen said, "Get Karzai to do a book! Give him a proposal. People would love to hear his story." I wrote a brief proposal, two pages, and gave it to Ludin to present to Karzai. After his commencement address at BU, the president and his entourage flew off to Washington, then out to Nebraska, where Karzai received another honorary degree, and finally back to Kabul. I heard nothing for more than a month. Then Ludin called. "The president wants to do the book. What do we do now?"

I arranged to take a leave of absence from BU, and flew to Kabul in mid-September. For the next three months, I lived in a humble guesthouse, Chez Ana, run by an old journalism friend, Edward Girardet. I met with President Karzai evenings when he could find the time. I never knew until a few hours before if we were to meet that evening. My cell phone would ring, and an aide would say, "His Excellency the President would like to see you this evening." At the appointed hour, a black Russian Lada sedan would pull up in front of Chez Ana and off I'd go to the palace, passing through the layers of security until I was inside the massive palace walls and then walking alone down the dark sidewalks to the president's office as armed men in the shadows spoke softly into lapel microphones. Once inside the Gulkhana, the president's office building, I would wait to be ushered into the Afghan equivalent of the Oval Office, to a hearty handshake and a warm greeting from President Karzai.

Often we would meet there in the office, which is a large, comfortable room, richly furnished with a leather sofa and chairs and the president's desk. At times there were aides, advisers, or even a cabinet minister present, and Karzai welcomed them to stay. He's a natural storyteller, as many Afghans are, and enjoys an audience. Sometimes we would meet alone, in which case the president liked to retire to a paneled den behind the office, where we would watch television news for a few minutes before getting to work. Typically on those chilly autumn evenings Karzai would be wrapped in a long cream-colored *patou*, the accessory blanket that many Afghan men carry. Central heating was virtually nonexistent in Afghanistan, even in the presidential palace.

We would drink coffee—Karzai preferred it to tea—accompanied by Afghan raisins, almonds, pistachios, grapes, and occasionally a plate of cookies or pastries, all set before us silently by a waiter from the presidential kitchen. Karzai would frequently boast of the quality of the Afghan produce, sounding like a Chamber of Commerce booster. "Try these!" he would command. "These [almonds, grapes, raisins] are the best!" And we would sit for a few minutes, chatting and prying open pistachios or munching grapes. Then I would turn on my tape recorder. I would suggest the topic for that night's discussion, and the president would start talking. He's a great talker, fluent and confident, and one is aware of his charisma and intellect, even one-on-one in informal settings.

One evening my afternoon phone call informed me that the president would like me to meet him at his residence, a spacious but modest two-story house within the palace grounds. Visiting there involved passing through a few additional layers of security, including at the gate leading inside the residence's walled compound and at the steel-plated front door of the house itself. Between the gate and the house was a circular drive, and within the circle was a garden with a small fishpond. One chilly November evening I found Karzai walking briskly around the garden, doing laps on the gravel driveway for fresh air and exercise, and I was invited to join him. It was difficult to keep up.

Inside the house, I would be shown into the foyer and then into the front room where the president receives guests. When we met in the residence, the room was often full of people, whom Karzai would greet effusively and who would then sit silently as I interviewed him. Occasionally he would call on one of his guests to support his recollection of a name or a date, and there would be discussion until all were agreed.

The meetings at home were almost always followed by dinner. The president would sit at the head of the long dining room table and seat me at his right hand. He would urge me to try this or that Afghan specialty, often dishing it onto my plate himself. *Pullao*, the delicious Afghan pilaf, was always on the table, along with vegetable dishes, fresh lettuce, tomatoes and radishes, and the Afghan flatbread *nan*. Small bottles of water were placed on the table for general consumption, and pomegranate juice was also served. There were never any women at the table—in keeping with Afghan tradition the women were kept out of the sight of visitors, and I never set eyes on any woman in the residence. The table talk was in Pashto and Dari, save for the occasional foray into English to address me. Dessert would be fresh fruit, perhaps accompanied by a pistachio-flavored pudding, and tea or coffee. These dinners ended at a fairly early hour, usually nine or nine thirty, and then I would be driven back to the guesthouse to transcribe my tapes and wait for the next call.

We concluded our sessions on December 18, and I flew home for Christmas and the lengthy process of turning the transcripts of those extraordinary evenings with Hamid Karzai into this volume.

Acknowledgments

The seeds that eventually sprouted into this book were planted twenty years ago in Peshawar, Pakistan. I am grateful to Boston University and Professor Joachim Maitre for sending me there as field director of the Afghan Media Project. And thanks to John Rendon for sending me to Kabul for the first time in 2004. For my early education about Afghanistan, I thank the students of the Afghan Media Resource Center; its director, Haji Sayed Daud; my "photo-j protégé," Abdul Wahab; my translators, Khalil and Osman; and my esteemed colleague and friend Stephen Olsson. Thanks to the former directors of the American Center in Peshawar, John Dixon and Richard Hoagland, for their hands-off support of the AMRC. My understanding of things Afghan and my enjoyment of life on the northwest frontier was enhanced considerably by friendships with the brilliant journalists Eddie Girardet and Donatella Lorch, who risked life and limb to cover the story of jihad; with Dr. Richard English and his partner-cum-wife, Chris Files; and with Dr. Laurance Laumonier of Médecins Sans Frontières, one of my life's heroes. Thanks, too, to the amazing Judy Grayson; to world traveler Kathy

Kaldor; to my brother, Peter, and sister, Lisa, for taking good care of my house in Maine during my lengthy stays in Afghanistan; and to my good friend Dr. Whitney Azoy, whose knowledge, both broad and deep, of Afghanistan's culture, language, geography, and personalities opened windows of understanding that would have remained closed to me. Whitney's erudite companionship and enthusiastic guitar playing and singing, and the presence of his beautiful wife, Ana, made the Kabul nights infinitely more pleasurable.

Among the important sources of knowledge that I tapped for broad background and specific detail are Ahmed Rashid's *Taliban: Militant Islam, Oil and Fundamentalism in Central Asia*; Steve Coll's *Ghost Wars*; George Crile's *Charlie Wilson's War*; *Soldiers of God*, by Robert D. Kaplan; *Afghanistan: A Short History of Its People and Politics*, by Martin Ewans; and the consistently excellent reporting on Afghanistan and Pakistan of Pamela Constable of the *Washington Post* and Carlotta Gall of the *New York Times*.

Thanks to superagent Helen Rees for her unswerving vision for this book, and for fearlessly flying off to Kabul to demonstrate her support. And I can't imagine working with a more supportive and perceptive editor than Hana Lane of John Wiley & Sons.

My most recent visit to Kabul was made all the more memorable by the friendships I shared with the revolving cast of Eddie Girardet's Chez Ana guesthouse, including Sally, Joanna, Zach, Vanessa, Laura, Norman, Marie, Carol, Anthony, and the rest.

Great thanks to Jawed Ludin, who as spokesperson for the president and then as chief of staff supported this book from the start. Jawed arranged my meetings with Hamid Karzai and provided the essential logistical support for my stay in Kabul. I also thank deputy spokesmen Khaleeq Ahmad and Hamed Elmi, and the staffs of the Office of the Spokesperson for the President and the president's Office of Protocol for their support and assistance.

Most of all, I thank President Hamid Karzai for the extraordinary opportunity to share evenings in the presidential palace with him, and to hear him tell his dramatic personal story. I hope that this book does his story justice, and that it helps readers gain a deeper understanding of a fascinating but endangered country, its fragile new democracy, and its complex and charismatic leader.

A Brief History of Afghanistan

T HE LAND known today as Afghanistan has been continuously inhabited by humans since the Stone Age, and there is archaeological evidence that early Afghans were among the first people to domesticate plants and animals. Afghanistan's earliest cities were among the ancient world's first urban centers, and during the Bronze Age (3000–2000 B.C.) the economy of Mundigak, near what is now Kandahar, was based on wheat, barley, sheep, and goats. During this period Afghanistan became the crossroads for migrations and trade between Mesopotamia and the East.

Starting at around 2000 B.C. Afghanistan became the home of Aryan tribes, giving rise to the country's ancient name of Aryana. The name is widely used today;

3

Afghanistan's national airline is called Ariana. Today's capital city of Kabul was established sometime during this era.

Darius the Great conquered most of Afghanistan and made it part of the Persian Empire in the period from around 522 to 486 B.C., but the Persians were the first to learn of the Afghans' hostility to foreign invaders as Persian rule was constantly challenged by tribal revolts. Alexander the Great, who conquered Persia and killed Darius to avenge his father's death, was the next conqueror to face the resistance of the Afghans when he swept into Afghanistan in 330 B.C. and made it part of the vast Macedonian Empire. His rule was also faced with constant revolts, and after four years of warfare he packed up his army and moved on into Central Asia. He returned to Afghanistan, conquered its major cities, and married a tribal chief's daughter, Rokhsana, before attacking India. Injured in India, Alexander died in Baluchistan at the age of thirty-two, but the Greek culture he brought to the region remained a powerful influence in Afghanistan for centuries to come. After Alexander's death, the country was divided up among four Greek governors, who eventually declared their independence from Greece and ruled for fifty-five years.

Buddhism was introduced into Afghanistan from India in the third century B.C. and flourished for hundreds of years, finding its greatest expression in the giant statues of Buddha carved in the fourth century A.D. into the high sandstone cliffs of Bamiyan. The statues stood in their niches for fifteen hundred years, surviving various assaults and defacements, including the near-total destruction of the city by Genghis Khan in the early thirteenth century, until they were blown to bits by the Taliban in 2001.

Islam arrived in Afghanistan from Arabia in the seventh century A.D., and over the next two hundred years much of the country was converted to Sunni Islam. Genghis

Khan's Mongol hordes conquered much of the Islamic lands of Central Asia in the early thirteenth century, but by the end of the century the Mongols themselves had converted to Islam. Today, 99 percent of Afghans are Muslims, about 80 percent Sunni and 19 percent Shia.

From the thirteenth to the eighteenth centuries, Afghanistan's territory and its important trade routes, including the famous Silk Road, were fought over and uneasily ruled by a succession of empires, dynasties, and warlords. The Ghaznavid Dynasty, which firmly established Islam in Afghanistan, rose in 962, lasted less than two hundred years, and was replaced by the Ghorids, who were driven out by Genghis Khan, only to reassert themselves a century later. Tamerlane ruled for thirty-four years; his successor, Buhlul, seized the Indian throne and founded the Lodi Dynasty, which was brought to an end when Babur, the founder of the Moghul Dynasty, took Kabul. There followed a parade of Afghan independence fighters, from Roshan to Khattak to Mir Wais and his son Mir Mahmud, who not only fought against foreign domination but invaded and conquered Persia, until the Persian leader Nadir Shah took back Persian lands and much of southern Afghanistan. In 1747, Nadir Shah was assassinated, the Persians were driven out, and modern Afghanistan was established under Ahmad Shah Durrani.

Durrani defeated the Moghuls in what is now Pakistan, threw the Persians out of Herat, and expanded Afghanistan's authority from Central Asia to Delhi and from Kashmir to the Arabian Sea. For nearly ninety years, Afghanistan was free of foreign domination but not of internal conflict, which was virtually constant under a succession of leaders until finally Dost Muhammad Khan was able to bring about near-complete Afghan unification. Then in 1839 the British invaded Afghanistan and installed a puppet king on the throne, a decision they would soon regret. The Afghan struggle against British rule, led by Akbar Khan, culminated in 1842 with the slaughter of the entire British garrison of Kabul and their dependents. Out of 4,500 soldiers and 12,000 or so camp followers, only one survivor reached the safety of the British fort in Jalalabad. Thus ended the first Anglo-Afghan War. Dost Muhammad Khan, who had been exiled by the British, returned to the throne.

In 1878 the British returned. They found Afghan resistance to be as stubborn as ever, but won a great deal of territory that the Afghans never recovered. In the famous battle of Maiwand in July 1889, an Afghan woman named Malalai won immortality by carrying the Afghan flag forward in battle after the soldiers carrying the flag had been killed by the British forces. Soon after, the British withdrew from Afghanistan, retaining the right to conduct its foreign affairs. This power resulted in the imposition of the Durand Line, which fixed the borders between Afghanistan and British India and split the Afghan tribal areas in two permanently, leaving half in what became Pakistan. Afghanistan also lost territories to the Russians in the north and west, before the Russians agreed in 1895 to fixed borders.

As Afghanistan entered the twentieth century and slowly began to modernize, the British tried a third time to conquer it, in 1921, and were again defeated. Afghanistan regained control of its foreign affairs, and Amanullah Khan declared himself king. He was overthrown in 1929, but the reign of his usurper, Habibullah Kalakani, was brief. He was assassinated by Nadir Khan, who was in turn assassinated in 1933. His son, Zahir Shah, ruled until 1973, when he was overthrown by Daoud Khan and the Afghan Communist Party. King Zahir Shah, who was vacationing in Italy when the coup occurred, stayed there until President Hamid Karzai brought him back to Kabul in 2002 to live out his days in the Arg Palace.

In 1978, Daoud was overthrown and killed in a Communist coup. Taraki became president, and began mass arrests, torture, and executions of suspected opponents. The mujahideen jihad against the Communist government began. The following year, 1979, Taraki was assassinated and Hafizullah Amin became president. U.S. ambassador Adolph Dubs was murdered in Kabul. A few months later, Amin was killed, and the Soviet Union invaded and installed Babrak Karmal as president. He was replaced by Dr. Najibullah in 1986.

In 1989, after ten years of a bloody insurgency by the Afghan mujahideen, the Soviet Union withdrew from Afghanistan. The mujahideen continued their fight against the Communist government of Najibullah, finally capturing Kabul in 1992 and forming the mujahideen government, headed by Professor Burhanuddin Rabbani. But vicious clashes among the mujahideen factions rendered the government unable to function, and in 1994 the Taliban movement was formed and began its march toward Kabul, seizing the capital in 1996 and executing Dr. Najibullah, who had been under UN protection since his ouster in 1992.

The Taliban's rule was marked by mass killings, torture, public executions, harsh treatment of women, and international condemnation. They also allowed the international terrorist group al-Qaeda, headed by the Saudi Osama bin Laden, to use Afghanistan as their base. The Taliban controlled most of Afghanistan, but never captured the northern areas held by the charismatic commander Ahmad Shah Massoud. Massoud's Northern Alliance was crucial to the defeat of the Taliban when the United States invaded Afghanistan in 2001 following the

A FEW FACTS ABOUT AFGHANISTAN*

Location:
  Southern Asia, north and west of Pakistan, east of Iran
Geographic coordinates:
  33° N, 65° E
Capital:
  Kabul (pronounced "cobble")
Provinces (34):
  Badakshan, Badghis, Baghlan, Balkh, Bamiyan,
  Daykondi, Farah, Faryab, Ghazni, Ghowr, Helmand,
  Herat, Jowzjan, Kabul, Kandahar, Kapisa, Khost, Konar,
  Kondoz, Laghman, Lowgar, Nangarhar, Nimruz,
  Nurestan, Oruzgan, Paktia, Paktika, Panjshir, Parwan,
  Samangan, Sar-e Pol, Takhar, Vardak, Zabul
Area:
  647,500 square kilometers (388,500 square miles);
  slightly smaller than Texas
Bordering countries:
  China 45.6 miles, Iran 561.6 miles, Pakistan 1,458 miles,
  Tajikistan 723.6 miles, Turkmenistan 446.4 miles,
  Uzbekistan 82.2 miles
Climate:
  Arid to semiarid; cold winters and hot summers
Terrain:
  Mostly rugged mountains; plains in north and southwest
Natural resources:
  Natural gas, petroleum, coal, copper, chromite, talc,

barites, sulfur, lead, zinc, iron ore, salt, precious and semiprecious stones

Population:
29,928,987 (July 2005 estimate)

Labor force:
Agriculture 80 percent, industry 10 percent, services 10 percent (2004 estimate)

Currency:
Afghani

Exchange rate:
$1 U.S. = 48 afghanis (approximate)

Adapted from The World Factbook

attacks on the World Trade Center and the Pentagon, attacks that had been planned in bin Laden's training camps in Afghanistan.

With the defeat of the Taliban, an interim government was formed with Hamid Karzai at its head. A coalition of international military forces provided security. An emergency *loya jirga*, or grand council, of Afghans chose Karzai as president of the transitional government in 2002, and he was elected president of the Islamic Republic of Afghanistan in democratic elections in 2004. A new constitution was created, parliamentary elections were held in 2005, and Afghanistan began what is sure to be a long and difficult road to peace, stability, and prosperity.

Introduction

PESHAWAR, PAKISTAN, in the 1980s had to be one of the most fascinating places on earth.

The capital of old India's, now Pakistan's, wild and woolly North-West Frontier Province, the ancient Pathan, or Pashtun, city had been the stopping place of countless camel caravans and conquering armies traversing the legendary Khyber Pass, twenty-five miles to the west, to and from Afghanistan. In the nineteenth century, the British army established a garrison in Peshawar and stretched a string of sentry posts high into the Hindu Kush mountains. One of the posts, from where the young Winston Churchill reported on a battle between British-led Hindu Sikhs and Pashtun tribesmen, is still known as Churchill's Picket.

Beginning with the Soviet Union's invasion of Afghanistan in 1980, Peshawar became the temporary home for thousands, then tens of thousands, then millions of Afghans who had fled their country to escape both Soviet Communist rule and the steadily escalating violence of the jihad, the Muslim "holy war" waged against the Soviets by ragtag militiamen called mujahideen, or "holy warriors."

The refugees settled in Peshawar's already teeming streets and in vast refugee camps, sizable towns themselves that sprang up on the unpopulated plains outside of town. The Afghans opened tiny shops in the narrow, crooked streets of Peshawar's old bazaars, selling heirloom family carpets and jewelry set with deep blue lapis lazuli stones from the famed mines of Badakshan. They also sold Soviet hammer-and-sickle military insignia and Red Army field caps, which came with often fanciful tales of how they had been plucked from the corpses of dead Russians. On the dusty plain outside of town Afghan horsemen played their wild games of *buzkashi* with calf carcasses.

The refugees attracted battalions of aid organizations, from the United Nations' World Food Program to the International Committee of the Red Cross to more obscure and sometimes dodgy enterprises that saw an opportunity to exploit the refugees' plight, raise pots of money from concerned Western donors, and live comfortably in one of Peshawar's large walled homes with servants to cook, clean, guard the gate, and do the laundry.

The chance to do battle with the Soviet Union through Afghan proxies roused the spirits of Western cold warriors, including President Ronald Reagan. Spurred by flamboyant Texas congressman Charlie Wilson, who adopted the jihad as his personal war, Reagan's administration financed weapons shipments and clandestine CIA operations on the side of the Afghan resistance. The CIA's supplying of Stinger shoulder-fired antiaircraft missiles to the mujahideen is often cited as a major factor in the eventual withdrawal of the Soviets from Afghanistan.

Shortly after their invasion the Soviets closed Afghanistan to Western journalists, who faced the risk of death when traveling inside the country with groups of armed mujahideen or the risk of arrest if they were caught. Countless tales of the horrors of imprisonment in Afghanistan's notorious Pul-i-Charkhi prison, or the chance of dying in a skirmish, deterred many journalists from even attempting a trip inside. That some did venture inside, such as the *Christian Science Monitor*'s Edward Girardet and the *New York Times*'s Donatella Lorch (who entered Kabul disguised in a burka), is a testament to their bravery and dedication to journalism.

The closing of Afghanistan made Peshawar an irresistible magnet for journalists from around the world, and as "going inside" was so hazardous and arduous, Peshawar became a thriving information bazaar. Every major faction of the Afghan resistance, and several minor ones, had headquarters there, and their spokesmen were eager to plant not only information but rumors, misinformation, disinformation, and gossip into the dispatches of Western journalists, many of whom were ignorant of the language, culture, and multilayered nuances of relations among the various families tribal groups and political parties. Every Afghan party published its own "newsletter," which contained romantic and usually inaccurate or wildly exaggerated descriptions of the victories of their mujahideen. Many journalists who were there for the long haul relied on the newsletter of Professor Sayeed Majrooh, a former Kabul University philosophy teacher whose Afghan Information Center was the most reliable of the many Afghan

sources. Dr. Majrooh was assassinated in 1988 by fundamentalists from the party of Gulbuddin Hekmatyar.

Peshawar was full of not only journalists, Afghan
refugees, commanders, and mujahideen, but also of every
shade of spy, saboteur, agent provocateur, and soldier of for-
tune imaginable. The town was often shaken by the boom
of terrorist bombs, and rare was the night without gunfire.
Spies from Pakistan's powerful intelligence agency, the ISI,
mingled with those of the Soviet Union's KGB; its Afghan
counterpart, KHAD; the American CIA; and Britain's MI6.
At the famous Green's Hotel, a shabby survivor from the
days of empire, one tableful of tea-drinkers could be seen
leaning with comical obviousness toward another table, ears
straining to pick up shards of whispered conversation.

This was the Peshawar to which I traveled in November
1986 to scout the ground for Boston University's Afghan
Media Project. On that first visit I hoped to get the Pakistani government's official permission to conduct the
project on Pakistani soil. Many meetings, handshakes,
and cups of tea later I realized no government official
would put his signature on the required document, which
in Pakistan is called a "certificate of non-objection," so I
decided we should just go ahead without permission and
see what happened. We found classroom space in
Peshawar's University Town, where most of the aid groups
and expats were located, and set about recruiting students
for our first training session, which was to last six weeks.
That's when I first met Hamid Karzai.

We made it a requirement from the start to recruit
equally from all of the major parties, so we began to make
the rounds of party headquarters explaining the project
and asking each party to send us a half dozen people to
be trained in video news gathering, photojournalism,
and print journalism. When we called on Professor

Mojaddedi's Afghan National Liberation Front, our contact was a poised, smiling, and immaculately groomed Hamid Karzai, then a young man of thirty years of age but already bald; his neatly trimmed beard was gray. Westerners especially liked to deal with Karzai because he was bright, personable, and pleasant, and his English eliminated the need for cumbersome and often suspect translation. He was also diplomatic and always spoke well of the other resistance parties, even though he had by now developed a strong aversion to the extreme Islamist practices of some of them, especially Gulbuddin Hekmatyar's faction of the Hezb-i-Islami party, the "Party of Islam." Karzai's moderate views, engaging personality, linguistic ability, and position in the ANLF put his name on invitation lists, and he often attended social functions at the U.S. consulate in Peshawar or the residence of John Dixon, the director of the U.S. Information Service's American Center and his successor, Richard Hoagland. While some Pakistani and Afghan guests took advantage of these gatherings to imbibe forbidden alcohol, Karzai quenched his thirst with tea or soft drinks.

After two training sessions, the Afghan Media Resource Center was established, staffed by the Afghans we had trained or recruited from the various parties. The AMRC was doing exactly what we had hoped for—augmenting the news coverage of a war that was very difficult for Western journalists to cover, and helping to open the world's eyes to what was happening inside Afghanistan. I left Peshawar at the end of August 1988 and did not see Hamid Karzai again for sixteen years.

In the intervening years the news from Afghanistan was, for much of the time, dismayingly bad. The jihad against the Soviet Union had been replaced by internecine warfare among the Afghan factions, warfare that damaged

Afghanistan far more than had the struggle to drive the U.S.S.R. from the country. The civil wars were finally quelled, in large measure, by a seemingly altruistic religious movement, the Taliban, which at first won the applause of the world for bringing peace at last to poor Afghanistan. The applause soon turned to dismay, shock, and horror as the Taliban's barbaric governance became known, and to anger when they hosted Osama bin Laden and his terrorist movement. Then came September 11, 2001, and the world collectively decided that the Taliban must go and that bin Laden must be stopped.

After the terrible shocks of that autumn, I was surprised and pleased to learn that my old Peshawar acquaintance Hamid Karzai had been picked by the UN-brokered Bonn Conference to be the head of a provisional Afghan government. Later he would be selected by a grand loya jirga, a traditional form of Afghan assembly, to be president of the interim government. Finally, in the fall of 2004, Karzai would be elected president of the Islamic Republic of Afghanistan, in that country's first ever democratic national election.

Throughout the period from the defeat of the Taliban to the election of Karzai, hope and optimism were palpable in Afghanistan. Released from the draconian grip of the Taliban, the country was exhuberant. Music played, men danced in public, couples married in newly opened wedding halls decked with plastic flowers, as there are few fresh flowers in Afghanistan. Bazaars overflowed with goods and shoppers, the dusty streets were clogged with traffic, restaurants opened, and new homes and office buildings sprang up like weeds, as did competing mobile-phone companies, privately owned radio stations, and independent newspapers. Karzai's approval ratings soared at home, and on his trips abroad the handsome, charismatic, and exotically garbed president was accorded rock-star status. His signature outfit, a long green cloak called a *chappan* and a lambswool cap, became a symbol of the new Afghanistan that Karzai and the entire world would help to build from the rubble of the failed state that had been taken over by fanatics and terrorists.

Afghanistan was back in the world.

Such euphoria couldn't last. Afghanistan's problems were myriad and massive, and the realities of the nation's plight began to take a toll on the collective optimism. Here was a desperately poor, war-shattered country that was being remade almost from scratch. Ethnic and tribal hostilities forged during decades of conflict would not be buried overnight. A completely new government had to be created, with functioning executive, legislative, and judicial branches. A completely new physical infrastructure was needed—roads, power plants, schools, water systems, all of which had been destroyed or badly damaged in the war years. None of this, it was clear, could be done in a hurry or on the cheap. And all of it would require a security force capable of giving Afghanistan a safe, stable environment in which to achieve its objectives. The United States and its NATO allies would provide this force. But, as it turns out, the force that has been provided has been, from 2001 onward, not nearly enough. Decisions made in the United States by the Bush administration have consistently undermined the security of Afghanistan and President Karzai's ability to deliver on the promise of a new Afghanistan.

Afghanistan can still be saved, but it is not at all certain that it will be. The Taliban, having found a safe haven in Pakistan, are resurgent. Osama bin Laden lives to plot future attacks on the United States and the West. The vast profits garnered by drug lords corrupt the government and weaken what little authority it has. Hamid Karzai, the putative savior of the nation, is a virtual prisoner in his Kabul palace. I believe Karzai was the right person to lead Afghanistan out of its Dark Ages. He is passionately Afghan and fervently believes in the Afghan nation. He is not corrupt. His heritage and education and the force of his personality allow him to bridge the East-West divide as perhaps no Afghan has ever done. But Karzai can't do it alone. Without a robust commitment by the United States and its allies, Afghanistan will again fail. If we do not pay the price for Afghanistan's success, we shall surely pay the price for its failure.

1

Hamid Karzai

I T WAS A VERY Afghan moment, just the sort of good news–bad news dichotomy that had plagued Afghanistan's recent history. In the 1980s, the Afghans had beaten the Soviet Union, but their efforts to govern their own country had devolved into years of ruinous internecine violence. In the mid-1990s, the Taliban had brought law and order, but only by the imposition of a medieval regime as harsh as anything the Spanish Inquisition ever dished up, and along with them had come a fanatic Saudi and training bases for international terrorism. The Afghans couldn't win for losing.

The date was December 5, 2001, less than three months after the al-Qaeda-sponsored attacks on New

York and Washington, D.C. The United States and Britain had begun to attack Afghanistan overtly, from the air, on October 7, although special forces from both countries had been conducting covert operations inside the country in advance of the bombing campaign, trying to organize the so-called Northern Alliance into a unified force to oust the Taliban. The Taliban branded the bombing "an attack on Islam." The objective of the United States and its allies was not only to unseat the odious regime of the Taliban, whom, incidentally, the United States had initially supported, but also to destroy the bases and training camps inside Afghanistan operated by al-Qaeda, the shadowy terrorist organization led by the wealthy Saudi Osama bin Laden. Meanwhile, an emergency conference had been convened in Bonn, Germany, to plan the shape of a post-Taliban Afghan government. Hamid Karzai, at that point the man most likely to head an interim Afghan government, had slipped into the southern part of the country shortly after 9/11 to rally the mostly Pashtun population of the area against the Taliban. With American airpower and Special Forces support, Karzai's small but growing force had been taking villages and towns one after another. On November 12, the Northern Alliance came down from the mountains and attacked Kabul, driving out the Taliban without firing a shot. Northern Alliance fighters entered the capital in triumph the following day, to a raucous welcome by the long-suffering citizens. The Taliban, in headlong flight in their hallmark white pickup trucks, had signaled that they were ready to surrender.

Karzai and a few dozen Afghan fighters, along with U.S. Special Forces advisers, were in a village called Shah wali Kot, just north of Kandahar. American planes were bombing a nearby ridgeline where a small Taliban force was firing intermittently at the village. The Afghan soldiers, a number of villagers, and some of the Americans had gone up a small hill at the edge of the village to watch the air strikes. Karzai had started up the hill when he was told by an aide that some elders from the area wanted to meet with him, so he turned back and entered a small house where the tribal leaders were seated. Suddenly a massive explosion shattered the windows of the house, blew off the door, and rained debris down on Karzai and the chiefs. A huge 2,000-pound satellite-guided bomb, dropped from an American B-52, had been directed to the wrong hilltop. Three Americans, at least two dozen Afghan soldiers, and a number of civilians were killed.

In the little house, an American soldier had thrown himself on Karzai, as had the tribal chiefs. They hustled him out of the rubble and into a sheltered area among some boulders where aides began to clean off the blood, dust, and debris from his head. Just then his satellite telephone rang. An aide answered. "English," he said, handing the phone to Karzai. It was the BBC's Lyse Doucet, calling from Bonn.

"Congratulations," she said. "You have been named head of the new interim Afghan government."

Another phone call came, from an Afghan commander in Kandahar who said that a senior Taliban delegation was en route to Shah wali Kot to deliver their letter of surrender to Hamid Karzai.

Hamid Karzai was born in December 1957 in Kandahar Province, Afghanistan. His name, Karzai, means that he is from the village of Karz, which is the ancestral seat of his family. Afghans do not usually note the exact date of a child's birth, nor do they celebrate birthdays, and many Afghans cannot even tell you in what year they were born, but the Karzais are an educated and prominent family.

Karzai's father was chief of the Popolzai tribe, as was his father before him. The Popolzais are a subtribe of the Abdalis, who ruled Afghanistan for more than two centuries, until King Zahir Shah was overthrown in 1973. Although Hamid Karzai himself became chief of the Popolzais upon the death of his father, who was assassinated by the Taliban in 1999, he preferred not to talk about tribes. "I am simply an Afghan," he said.

The Karzai family was very close to the king, and one of Hamid's first acts as president of the interim government was to bring the king back to Kabul from his long exile in Italy and install him in comfortable quarters in his former palace, surrounded by friends and family.

Karzai is one of eight children—he has six brothers and one sister—and in age he is roughly in the middle. "We are an educated family," he said, "but conservative and traditional. We were not rich; there were many families in Kandahar who were far wealthier." But the family was prominent by virtue of its long history and close ties to the ruling families, and so was privileged by Afghan standards, living a comfortable life in a large walled compound. While his father was a powerful khan, Karzai remembers his mother as a very spiritual person who fasted often. "I learned a great deal about high moral standards from her," he said.

Karzai was born in the last—and one of the few— peaceful periods in Afghan history. The king was on his throne, ruling benignly over a loose federation of tribes that included the populous Pashtuns in the south, Tajiks and Uzbeks in the north, and Shiite Hazaras, long the persecuted minority, in the center. Although Karzai spent the first few years of his life in Karz, and began his schooling there, after his first year of school the family moved to Kabul. Karzai's father had been elected to the parliament, which met in Kabul during what Afghan historians refer to as the Decade of Democracy. The government of Zahir Shah was a constitutional monarchy, and the elections for parliament were conducted just as democratic elections are today. The candidates campaigned both for themselves and their like-minded friends who were also standing for election by making speeches, hosting lunches for voters—the normal repertoire of political campaigners. The senior Karzai was then in his forties.

Kabul in those days was a clean, orderly, and fairly cosmopolitan city, with broad tree-lined avenues. It was a favorite posting for Western diplomats, who found themselves awed by the spectacular Hindu Kush mountains and enchanted by the rough-and-ready Afghans, whose culture and customs seemed to spring straight out of the days of Genghis Khan, especially in the villages beyond Kabul. Photographs from those days picture a capital enjoying a tranquility that was soon to be shattered, government officials wearing Western suits, and modern, well-appointed ministry buildings.

Kabul was also a destination for wanderers, adventurers, and hippies, who found Afghanistan's opium potent and affordable and the country's attitudes toward drugs laissez-faire. Afghanistan's poppies were well-known to the drug culture of Europe, but the era of wealthy and powerful drug lords, their heroin factories and worldwide export channels, was still a few years away.

While Afghanistan had a monarch and a parliament, much of the work of government was done at the provincial and village levels, and much of Afghanistan's political power was vested not in elected officials or even in the monarchy but in local khans. There was a government in Kabul, to be sure, but tradition ruled the countryside. Many things were done, many issues were settled in traditional Afghan ways that go back hundreds of years and for which there is nothing written down. Karzai recalls how his father would settle local disputes on the strength of his role as tribal chief, not from any powers he derived from being an elected official.

"My father was often called upon to settle disputes," Karzai told me. These might be disputes over land, property, water, marriage, or any number of things. Depending on how major the issues are, they may be settled by a sub-chief or they may require a group of important chiefs. Testimony is heard from all the affected parties, a decision is made by the chief, and that's that. No paperwork is issued, no signatures are required, but the verdict sticks. Daily life in the Karzai household was full of such business.

Afghan homes have a guest room, where visitors can meet with the head of the house and his sons, drink tea, and munch on almonds or grapes or even take meals, while the rest of the family, especially the women, remain out of sight. Unless the visitor is a close relative, he will never see any part of the home but the guest room. The guest section of the Karzai house was entirely used for local politics—the settling of disputes, the granting of favors, the arrangement of marriages.

Sometimes the dispute was on a larger scale, involving too many people for the khan to receive the disputing parties in his guest room, so the elder Karzai and other chiefs would travel to a village to settle things. Karzai remembers one land dispute that required all the heavyweights of Kandahar to settle. Hamid accompanied his father to this event, in a village called Neesh, which is located between Kandahar and Oruzgan, probably as part of the education of a young man who might one day become chief of the tribe. For the village, this was a major event, and at least a hundred people from the area had gathered, some to give testimony and others just to gawk at the visiting chiefs and wait for the outcome. Both sides of the dispute presented their arguments, and Karzai's father and the other chiefs listened carefully. Then the chiefs huddled by themselves and discussed the case. "When they had arrived at a decision," Karzai said, "they called the two sides together and told them, 'This is how it will be.' Both sides accepted the decision, and that settlement stands to this very day."

The power of Afghan tradition, on full display that day, sufficiently impressed the young Karzai that he remembers the occasion well even now. But he was given another reason to remember it. The Karzais were guests of the village's most prominent family, "a very spiritual family," Karzai recalled, who still reside in that village. The host family's status was enhanced by a stable of handsome horses. Afghans are legendary equestrians, and greatly prize their horses, which are bred for quickness, endurance, and courage.

All these traits are on display in buzkashi, the closest thing the Afghans have to a national sport; its greatest players are the northern tribesmen. Buzkashi—the literal translation of the word is "goat grabbing"—in its purest form is played without teams on the open plains. A goat or a calf is sacrificed, beheaded, and disemboweled, then the carcass is laid on the ground. The horsemen—and in the old, freeform days there might have been fifty or even a hundred—clenching their short, brutal, wood-handled whips in their teeth when not beating their own horse or someone else's, try to maneuver their mounts into position over the dead goat, producing a wild scrum of plunging, whinnying, biting horses. In the midst of the madness, a rider will reach down, hooking one leg around the saddle and the other under the horse's belly, grasp the seventy-five-pound carcass, lift it off the ground, and try to ride away with it, while other riders pursue and try to wrestle the carcass away. To score a point, the horseman with the carcass must ride "free and clear" of all pursuers. Sometimes this scrimmage will culminate with two riders each holding a leg of the unfortunate goat as their horses race at full gallop over the plains. Such is the strength of the men that often a leg will be ripped from the carcass, leaving one rider victorious and the other holding a leg of goat. In more recent times, the contestants have been divided into teams and the matches confined to a soccer stadium. This is somewhat safer for spectators, who on the open plains often had to run for their lives as the seething herd bore down on them, but the freedom and individuality of the old game is lost.

The buzkashi was a formal, elaborately arranged event that took place over a number of days. A khan who felt he had the wealth and the power to stage one would plan for weeks. Invitations would be issued, food would be stored, sleeping quarters would be arranged, and the best players would be invited to participate. Should the khan be snubbed by an important invitee or a star horseman, or if he failed to provide adequate food and shelter for his guests, or if fighting broke out among rival clans, or if the prize money was insufficient, he would lose status and power.

This buzkashi mentality—do not attempt to use or display your authority unless you're sure you can pull it off, or risk losing what authority you possess—informs and influences the entire process of Afghan governance, and would influence Karzai himself after his rise to power. As president of a newly democratic Afghanistan, Hamid Karzai is acutely aware of the limits of his power and doesn't attempt what he knows he can't accomplish. This has been evident in his dealings with various warlords—some of whom he has succeeded in removing from their power bases—and with the country's drug production, which he knows he is powerless to halt at present.

Back at the village of Neesh, as Karzai and his father were taking tea with their hosts in the village, someone brought one of the family's horses around for them to admire. Young Hamid decided he wanted to ride this horse, although he had never ridden before. He got on the beast and managed to make it move, then rode it slowly a short distance away from the village. "So far, so good," he recalled with a wry smile. "But when I turned the horse's head back toward the village, he took off running at a full gallop, eager to get back to his home." This being his first time on a horse, Karzai didn't know how to stop him, and so he just hung on for dear life. The horse ran straight for his stable. As he went through the stable door, Karzai had the presence of mind to grab the crossbeam over the door. The horse ran right out from under him, and he hung there in the stable doorway and then dropped to the ground, unhurt. "That was scary," Karzai said. "Everyone rushed to see that I was all right, and one old man of the village said to me, 'Very good! You're a clever boy.'" Later, as the Karzais were leaving the village, a man came up to them leading a "beautiful little horse" and presented it to Hamid as a gift. "I named it Guli Badam, which means almond blossom, because of its light brown coat with small white spots that looked like the petals of the almond flower," Karzai said. He kept the horse for many years, and often thinks of that incident as an example of the Afghan character and tradition that he reveres. Despite his country's brutal history and the Afghans' reputation as fierce and unforgiving warriors, Karzai believes in the essential generosity and hospitality of his people.

Indeed, the code by which many Afghans, most famously the Pashtuns, live is comprised of the triad of honor, hospitality, and revenge. An Afghan is obliged to extend hospitality to all under his roof, even an enemy. But any insult to honor must be avenged; there is simply no choice in the matter. Karzai's father and other chiefs, in rendering decisions and settling tribal matters, understood that the honor of each side in a dispute must emerge intact.

In Kandahar, the Karzais lived in a substantial house with a large garden. The family compound was large enough that Hamid could ride his horse inside the walls. The garden had fishponds, trees, and flowers, and he remembers there being many birds. His memories are of a comfortable life but a very disciplined one. The standards of behavior were quite rigid, but it was "an upbringing that has served me well in my life," Karzai said. "We learned to respect and obey not only our parents, but our elders in general. That's a very Afghan way of life and it's especially strong in the countryside."

After he became president, Karzai invited a provincial governor to meet with him in his office in the Arg, the presidential palace in Kabul, and the governor brought his little son with him. The boy was about two and a half years old. When the father and his son entered the presidential office, Karzai immediately picked up the boy in his arms and said hello, giving him a hug and a kiss. "But he had a job that he had been trained to do," Karzai said, "and this little boy didn't forget it even though I had thrown him off the track with my greeting." The boy had already learned from his family that he must kiss the hand of an elder as soon as he is introduced, and Karzai had not given him a chance to do this. But as soon as the president set the little fellow down, he said hello—*Salaam aleikum*—and took Karzai's hand and kissed it. "Then he felt that he had properly done his job," Karzai said. "That is how we were raised. In the traditional Afghan family, children are taught to be very respectful of elders."

The young Hamid Karzai was a quiet boy and gained a small circle of friends after the family moved to Kabul. "Two small circles, actually—one at school and one in my neighborhood," he said. Each of the friends had to be approved by the families before the boys could visit one another's homes. The boys' parents always knew where their children were and whom they were with. Even as teenagers the Karzai children had to ask for their parents' permission to go places, such as the cinema. "I didn't hang out with my siblings a lot because of age differences," Karzai said, "but sometimes we would gather up relatives—cousins and aunts and uncles—to go to the cinema." Hamid and his friends also liked to play soccer and to go bicycling around the town.

Some of Karzai's favorite memories are of family outings to Istalif, a small village about an hour's drive from Kabul that is famous for its potters and greenery and that attracts city families to this day for picnics or weekend getaways. Istalif was later badly damaged in the fighting in 2001, but in those times it was a green and pleasant resort village, like an oasis, with streams and pools, orchards and forests. Many of its families earn a living producing handmade pottery with distinctive green and blue glazes, which can be found in markets all over the country. Once a year one of Karzai's maternal uncles, who was head of the government printing house, would host a grand party in Istalif. "All the kids in the extended family would be there, all of my cousins, with their parents and grandparents, and we would stay for three or four days, running around, climbing trees, playing in the streams," Karzai said. "Those outings were the most fun times of my childhood."

As a child of privilege, the young Karzai was perhaps a bit too full of himself, and he remembers being taken down a peg during one outing in Istalif. His uncle had brought an Afghan singer named Natou to perform. Natou was famous throughout Afghanistan for his singing of traditional songs. Hamid, who was "nine or ten at the time," sat down beside him and listened and watched. When Natou had finished singing a song, Karzai said, "Sir?" The old singer looked down at him and said, "Yes, my boy?" Hamid, thinking to show off his knowledge of Afghan music, asked him, "Can you sing a classical song?" He was referring to the ragas, like classical Indian ragas, which were also played in Afghanistan. "But that was like asking a country folk musician to play Beethoven," Karzai said, "and Natou got very angry with me. 'Get away from me!' he growled. 'What do you know about classical music?'"

Karzai remembers Kabul in that time as not only clean, safe, and "quite chic," but as the seat of a well-functioning government. After he had gone off to India to university— this was after the overthrow of the king—he returned to Kabul for his first winter vacation and was struck by how much more efficient and well-administered things were as soon as he traveled from Pakistan into Afghanistan. Crossing into Pakistan, all the passengers had to get off the bus and line up to go through passport control. But when the bus returned to Afghanistan, the passengers remained seated while a policeman came aboard to collect passports. The foreigners' passports were brought back to them on the bus, but Karzai was told that his Afghan passport would be kept there at the border and sent on to Kabul, where he would be able to collect it at the Foreign Ministry. "Sure enough, when I went to the ministry a week later my passport was there waiting for me," Karzai said. "I was proud that the Afghan administrative system was more efficient." And after traveling by bus through

India and Pakistan, Kabul looked to the young Karzai almost like a European city. Almost everyone wore Western clothing. Photographs from that time support his recollection. There were not many automobiles, but the city had a very good public transportation system, with electric and diesel buses going to all neighborhoods. The Kabulis were quite worldly, and Western influences were apparent. "You could hear the latest music being played—Tom Jones, Engelbert Humperdinck," Karzai said. He liked to frequent a music shop called the Afghan Music Center, which was owned by a family friend, where he would sit in a little cubicle with headphones on and listen to music before deciding whether to buy it. There were also many good restaurants.

The Afghan classrooms of Karzai's early education were places of learning and also of very strong discipline. The classroom played a very important role in shaping the youth of Afghanistan. "We greatly respect teachers," he said. "No matter how bad you might be outside of school with your friends, the moment you saw a teacher, and not just your own but any teacher, you would straighten up and behave yourself."

Hamid liked school "very, very much" at first. But that was before the coup that ousted Zahir Shah and ushered in Communism. In 1973, while the king was traveling in Italy, the former prime minister, Mohammed Daoud Khan, a cousin and brother-in-law of the king, seized power. As prime minister, Daoud Khan, though not a Communist, had been forging strong links with the Soviet Union and had received large quantities of military supplies, including modern weapons. In plotting a comeback, Daoud had also managed to play off the two Afghan Communist parties, the Parchams and the Khalqs, who had been agitating against the monarchy, and had many allies in the military establishment as well. Daoud's coup was at first welcomed by the U.S.S.R., but he was essentially an Afghan patriot, well to the right of Communism, who believed in a strong one-party central government and centrally controlled economic development.

The Communists who had helped Daoud seize power enjoyed newfound status in the Kabul government, and their influence extended into Afghan schools, including Habibia High School, the largest and best of the city's secondary schools, where Hamid Karzai was enrolled. "We began getting some Communist teachers," Karzai said, "and they were after some people. I was not aware that a teacher could have a grudge against someone like me, but I remember a Communist biology teacher who had it in for me because he thought I lived a privileged life. He had crazy ideas and thought that in my house all we had to do was push a button and food would come out of the kitchen on a rail." One day the tenth-grader Hamid Karzai challenged the biology teacher's ideas about the evolution of man. "It was a subject I had done a lot of reading on, Darwinian theory and all that, and I realized that I knew more than this teacher knew," Karzai said. "When I challenged him he almost beat me. That was the only time I ever got into trouble at school."

The coup of 1973 changed a lot of things, including Karzai's family life. His father came under pressure because of his close association with the king, an association that a few years later would lead to his imprisonment in the notorious Pul-i-Charkhi prison, where over the years the Communists sent thousands of political prisoners, many to be tortured and killed.

When Karzai graduated from Habibia High School, he made the decision to study in India. The coup, and the introduction of Communist teachers, may have influenced his choice, but his brothers were also a factor. Two of them were studying in the United States, and they urged Hamid to go where he could learn English. He had grown up speaking two languages, Pashto and Dari, which is also called Farsi, the Afghan variety of Persian. Both languages were spoken interchangeably in the Karzai home, which, Karzai says, illustrates a very important aspect of the Afghan character. Kabul, and other Afghan cities as well, was a melting pot, where people from all over the country came together. "And in the making of the educated Afghan character, both languages were spoken and both languages were equally Afghan—there was no distinction," Karzai said. "Nobody thought of Pashto as the language of only the Pashtuns and Farsi as the language of some other groups. No. They were the languages of Afghanistan. That's a very important point. We are bilingual but unicultural."

Karzai offered another example of Afghan's uniculturalism. "Recently a friend of mine from Zabul came to see me," he said. "His appearance—his chappan, his turban, his overall dress—and his manners and the way he spoke were not in the slightest any different from the appearance and manners and speech of another good friend from Badakshan. And those places are more than a thousand kilometers apart." And the further back you go in Afghan history, Karzai claims, the less difference you would see from place to place. Karzai's father, from Kandahar, wore a karakul hat. So did another khan, Mahanyar, from the Hazarajat, and other men from elsewhere in the country. "Same hats, same manners," Karzai said. "The best book on the Afghan loya jirgas was written by a man from the north, not from the south where the loya jirgas have taken place," he said. "We are all Afghans."

A lot of young Afghans were going to India to study at that time, and a maternal cousin of Karzai's had gone to Delhi to study medicine. (He is now a leading cancer specialist in the United States.) Karzai went to Delhi but quickly found that he could not tolerate the oppressive heat. After all, he had been living in Kabul, which sits at an altitude of around six thousand feet, and where even in the middle of summer the climate is agreeable. Delhi was simply too hot for him. His cousin suggested that he travel to Simla, in the hills, where there was a university, Himachal Pradesh University. Karzai remembers the train ride from Delhi to Simla as "almost magical. We left the heat of the city behind, and the train rolled through beautiful countryside as it climbed into the hill country. Blossoms from the trees beside the rails tumbled into the car as the train brushed up against the branches, and clouds seemed to pass right in one window and out another." Simla had been a major hill station, where the families of British officers and high-ranking administrators went in the summer to escape the heat of the cities. The British liked it so much they made it the summer capital of India. Karzai was enchanted. "I thought it was wonderful," he said. "The scenery was magnificent, with snowy mountaintops, and the climate was very much to my liking." He applied to the university, and although it would not recognize his diploma from Habibia High School, he was accepted, the first Afghan to enroll there.

The first several months at the university were very difficult for Karzai, as he was the lone Afghan, separated from his family and friends, and the classes were taught in English—a language he did not yet speak. "It was a much harder life than the one I had led in Kabul," he said. At first he stayed at a guesthouse, a palatial Georgian "cottage" in Summer Hill, in the western part of town, where

Mahatma Gandhi stayed during his many visits to Simla. Later the mansion became the guesthouse of the All India Institute of Medical Sciences. "The place was lovely, but it offered no food or even tea, and it was more than an hour's walk from my college," Karzai said. "When I returned from my classes, I would walk into the hills to a hut where some construction workers took their meals, and I would eat there. The food was not very good and often had sand in it." After this humble supper Karzai would return to his room and study his textbooks.

He was forced to learn English as he went along. He also discovered that his Afghan education had not prepared him well for the lab exercises in the sciences. In terms of a general education, of science theory, and of world knowledge, he felt he was "miles ahead" of most of the Indian students. "We were tops in mathematics, in physics, in chemistry—all the formulas, the elements, we knew these by heart," he said. "We had also studied American history, the Napoleonic Wars, current affairs, and I knew far more about those things, and about the Amazon and the Mississippi, for example, than my Indian counterparts. But when it came to science lab practicals, they were massively ahead of me." Theories, the young Karzai understood perfectly. But the moment he entered a lab he was lost. He found the class in botany especially difficult in that first term. Those freshman difficulties in Simla led to something of a crusade in Karzai's later life; as president he has spoken many times at conferences of the need to correct the basics of the Afghan education, "so that there is a better balance of the general and the practical."

Karzai's first-term class in the English language was also difficult for him. Then one of his teachers—"a wonderful man"—saw that he was having difficulty and asked him what he was using for a dictionary. Karzai told him he was using a Farsi-English dictionary. The professor shook his head and said, "No, don't use that one. You will never learn. Pick up an all-English dictionary." So Karzai went to a shop and purchased a large dictionary, published by Random House, for thirty rupees—about two dollars at the time. After his meals in the evening he would go to his room and pick up his books. When he came to a word he didn't know, he would go to the dictionary. "And in the dictionary definition there would be more words that I didn't know, and I would look them up as well," he said. So in an evening he would fill five or six pages of a notebook with words and their definitions in simple language. "I did this for two or three months, and it was very difficult," Karzai said. "But when I went down to Delhi to apply for an extension of my housing, the Afghan boys I knew there were surprised to hear me speaking English. I hadn't even noticed, but I had picked up English in two or three months."

When Karzai returned to Simla he stayed in a hotel run by a widow and her two daughters, one Karzai's age and the other a little older. The father had passed away. "It was a very good family, and my conversations there helped tremendously in my learning of English," he said. He also noticed differences between Indian and Afghan families. "The Afghan families tend to try to live beyond their means. They overconsume. Everything is taken to excess. They put too much food on the table, they spend money they don't have on clothes, and there is no saving mentality. That's a strange characteristic of Afghans."

The university continued to advance Karzai from one level to the next, but still they did not accept his Habibia diploma and would never tell him what grades he had earned. It was only when he finished his undergraduate studies and enrolled in the master's program that the university finally recognized the high school diploma and told him what his grades had been for the past three years. Only then did he discover that he had failed his first-term English-language class but had passed everything else and been allowed to advance.

In 1978, Karzai went home to Kabul for another winter vacation, and while he was there Daoud Khan, the man who had overthrown the king and abolished the monarchy, was himself overthrown and killed in a bloody Communist coup. Karzai was at a friend's house near the Arg Palace when the shooting started and Daoud's opponents laid siege to the palace.

Since Daoud had overthrown the king, with the support of the Afghan Communist parties, he had moved gradually to the right and had purged most of the Communists from his government. He had also moved to wean Afghanistan away from its nearly total reliance on the U.S.S.R for economic and military support, turning south to India and west to Iran and the Arab countries. This trend caused considerable worry in Moscow, which had long viewed Afghanistan as a key to reinforcing Soviet influence in West Asia against the encroachments of China and as a stepping-stone to the Indian Ocean. The Soviets continued to cultivate clandestine relationships within the Afghan military, for use when the need arose. Daoud had also lost the support of part of his Pashtun base because of his softening stand on the hot-button issue of Pashtunistan, the ancestral lands of the Pashtuns that had been arbitrarily divided by the British in 1893 with the Durand Line. With the partition of India in 1948, what had been the Indian portion of Pashtunistan went to Pakistan. Daoud had earlier sided with those favoring a united Pashtunistan, which naturally angered the Pakistanis, but by 1978 he had backed away from his earlier stand and mended fences with Islamabad.

On April 27, 1978, with the backing of the Soviet Union, a tenuously united coalition of the Khalqi and Parchami parties attacked the palace, killing Daoud and most of his family. "Daoud Khan stood heroically against the Communists," said Karzai. "It is said that he was holding the Afghan flag as he faced them." The spot where he was killed is just inside the entrance to the Gulkhana, the stately honey-stone building where Hamid Karzai presides over the day-to-day business of his country. Karzai walks past the spot every day as he arrives, under heavy escort even within the palace walls, to begin the day's work. The physical traces of the assassination have long since vanished, but the mere knowledge of the event serves as a reminder to the president that very few Afghan leaders have left office alive.

The 1978 coup ushered in long years of misery for Afghanistan. The new Communist leaders brushed aside centuries of Afghan tradition and life. They attacked and oppressed everyone in the old order—the educated, the clergy, the tribal chiefs, the landed gentry. They moved violently against everyone whom they suspected of opposing them, as well as many they did not suspect. "Thousands and thousands of people were killed, and the Communists boasted about it!" Karzai said. "They put up lists on the walls of buildings with the names of people they had killed, twelve thousand people. They announced it! And that laid the foundation for the devastation of Afghanistan."

2

The Beginning
of Jihad

H AMID KARZAI had always been politically aware, because of his father's involvement with politics and his family's history and close friendship with the ruling family. At a very young age the senior Karzai had been a district administrator, and then chairman of the Chamber of Commerce for Kandahar. In Hamid's early years there were naturally some political discussions at home, but he said he never argued with his father about politics. In later times, during the anti-Soviet jihad and after, the Karzais and their political circle had many intense and endless discussions of politics within the decision-making members of the party. "I found myself to be quite headstrong, politically, and I would be the one who wanted quick action," Karzai said. "I develop strong convictions, and I'm driven by them, and when I feel something is right I will fight for it." Karzai thinks he inherited that aspect of his character partly from his father, but a very large part of it came from his mother and her strong moral convictions. Soon, Hamid Karzai's political convictions would begin to rule his life.

After the 1978 coup, when Karzai left Afghanistan to return to the university in Simla, communication with his family was very difficult, and no telephone calls were possible. The turmoil in Afghanistan continued. Then word reached him that his father had been taken prisoner by the Communist government, which was headed at the time by Nur Muhammad Taraki. The elder Karzai had been imprisoned, along with one of Hamid's uncles, in the infamous Pul-i-Charkhi prison. "It was only by chance and the will of God that he survived," Karzai said. "Many of the Afghans who were put into that prison did not come out alive." This was a very hard time for the young Karzai, knowing that his father and uncle were in that terrible prison and having no way to contact his family. He tried to follow the news of events in Afghanistan as well as he could and hoped for the best. Instead, things got worse.

Within months of seizing power from Daoud, Taraki was himself murdered. His killer and successor, Hafizullah Amin, held the reins only slightly longer. He was killed on Christmas Day of the following year in still another coup—one that would profoundly alter Afghan history and set off political tremors around the globe.

Karzai was then in postgraduate studies in Simla, working toward a master's degree in political science, and it was toward the end of his first postgraduate term that his life, along with the lives of millions of Afghans, was upended. In late December 1979, as he was walking to the campus, he overheard two girls talking excitedly. He picked up the word "Afghanistan" and tuned in to the conversation. "What I heard utterly changed my world," Karzai said. It was Christmas Day 1979, and the Soviet Union had invaded Afghanistan, killing Hafizullah Amin, seizing control of the government, and installing their handpicked puppet, Babrak Karmal, as the new Afghan leader. The Soviet invasion touched off a cold war crisis; U.S. president Jimmy Carter responded by strengthening ties to Pakistan and pulling American athletes out of the 1980 Moscow Olympic Games.

Upon hearing the news, Karzai's first instinct was to leave school and join the Afghan opposition in the fight to regain their homeland. "But after much thought and reflection, I concluded that the most useful thing for me, and for my country, would be to stay in India to complete my studies," he said.

The chain of dramatic events that began in 1973 with the overthrow of the monarch gave rise to an insurgent movement that became known as the mujahideen, or "holy warriors," a movement that was itself split broadly between Afghan traditionalists and Islamists. These groups variously disapproved of the ouster of the king, or of Daoud's somewhat westernized religious tolerance, or of Amin's and Taraki's Communism, or of some combination of these. And none approved of the Soviet interference. Each subsequent event following the overthrow of Zahir Shah seemed to fan the flames higher. Taraki's brutal brand of Communism and his harsh repression of dissenters drove many Afghans to flee the country into Pakistan or Iran, where they swelled the ranks of the mujahideen. When Hafizullah Amin seized power, his brutality exceeded even Taraki's and helped further strengthen the rebels. This alarmed the Soviets, who were investing heavily in Afghanistan by this time and wanted to control events there. The Soviets feared an Islamic fundamentalist backlash that could spread to the largely Islamic states on the U.S.S.R.'s southern border—Tajikistan, Uzbekistan, Turkmenistan, Kyrgyztan—and began making plans to oust Amin and install the more moderate and pliable Babrak Karmal, whom Taraki had sent off to Czechosolvakia as its ambassador to get him out of Kabul.

In February 1979, U.S. ambassador to Afghanistan Adolph Dubs, a noted expert on the U.S.S.R, was kidnapped on his way to work in Kabul by men dressed as Afghan police. He was taken to the Kabul Hotel and held while his kidnappers demanded the release of certain prisoners. American negotiators were trying to persuade Afghan authorities not to storm the hotel room when shooting erupted. Dubs was killed; three of the kidnappers survived. The United States, which had been giving only limited assistance to Afghanistan at the time, took steps to shut off the tap completely. A Soviet role in the murder of Ambassador Dubs was suspected but never proved definitively.

Ten months later, the Soviets' planning culminated in the invasion of December 25, 1979.

In Pakistan, the resistance to Afghanistan's Communist regimes grew by leaps and bounds with each successive government. Tens of thousands, then hundreds of thousands, and then, after the Soviet invasion, millions of Afghans fled their country. At the height of the Afghan-Soviet war, some four million Afghans were refugees in Pakistan, Iran, and elsewhere—the largest refugee group in world history. The feelings within Hamid Karzai to quit school and join the resistance assumed near-violent proportions.

After the Soviet invasion, the young Afghans studying in India were offered a chance by the U.S. government to go to the United States. Because some of Karzai's brothers were already in America, he went to the U.S. embassy in Delhi and filled in the required forms. He was told that because of his family he had a very strong case and would certainly be allowed to go to the United States. But Karzai decided against it. "Because I felt I could not stay in touch with events in Afghanistan as much as I wanted by being in India, I prepared to visit the Afghan refugee camps in Pakistan in the spring of 1980," he said. He and a cousin went first to Peshawar and from there to Quetta and spent a month visiting Afghan refugees and talking with them, seeing the conditions they were living in. He returned to Simla determined to finish his degree and then immediately go back to join the resistance.

Karzai's schooling was not free, and by this time his father had been imprisoned, leaving the family in Afghanistan somewhat in disarray. But financial help came from another family member. "I owe much to one of my brothers who was in the United States working as a waiter in a restaurant in Chicago," Karzai said. "He could not have been making very much money, but every month my brother sent me a letter with a check for a hundred dollars to pay for my school expenses. He later went on to open his own restaurant, and then others, and did very well."

After the Soviet takeover, the newly installed puppet government of Babrak Karmal freed many of the political prisoners jailed under Taraki and Amin as a goodwill gesture. Karzai's father and uncle were among them, although they were not in the first wave of prisoners released. They had to sit in cells in Pul-i-Charkhi prison for a few weeks more, perhaps due to their close ties to the monarchy. Once freed, the elder Karzai went directly from Afghanistan to Saudi Arabia to perform his hajj, the pilgrimage to Mecca that is the duty of all Muslims to undertake at least once in their lives. He went from there to Quetta, Pakistan, to assume a leadership role in the resistance with the Afghan National Liberation Front (ANLF), the party of his friend Professor Sibghatullah Mojaddedi. Other members of the family left Afghanistan one or two at a time, some going to the United States and others to stay in Pakistan.

Hamid was awarded his graduate degree in the winter of 1982. "My years at the university had been well spent," he said, "but now I was ready to join my father and my Afghan brothers in the resistance and do my part in the fight to regain Afghanistan for the Afghan people."

At the start of 1983, Karzai left Simla and headed for Quetta. During that forty-eight-hour journey, by a combination of trains and buses, "economy class the whole way," he first became aware of "a very disturbing development in the struggle of the Afghan people against the Communist Soviet occupation," he said. What he encountered was Islamic extremism.

On one leg of the trip, Karzai overheard some other young Afghan men on the same train, men of about his own age, talking about the jihad, the fight against the Soviets. They were from Hezb-i-Islami, which means "Party of Islam," one of the most radical of the Afghan resistance parties. As they talked, Karzai became aware of another dimension to the Afghan struggle, one that made him very uncomfortable. "I became aware of a political and ideological movement that wanted to undermine the traditional Afghan value system and the Afghan way of life." All forms of civil government would be replaced by a fundamentalist theocracy, and all law would flow from their extreme interpretation of the Holy Koran. The young men on the train were also saying that their way was the only way, that "every other element of the Afghan resistance, that every other person in the whole country, was worthless," Karzai said. Their thinking was the antithesis of the Afghan patriotism that had been central to Hamid Karzai's life. The conversation on that train was his first exposure to radical Islam, but certainly not the last.

"Over the months and years to come, I would see that this radical movement had many fathers," Karzai said. "Everyone had a hand in its growth—the West, the neighbors, everyone. And this movement was ultimately the cause of so much evil in Afghanistan, and so much destruction in the United States and the rest of the world."

When President Karzai speaks of "the neighbors," he generally is referring to only one neighbor: Pakistan. "The neighbors" would come up many times in conversations with him, as would his obvious frustration with the fact that a fellow Muslim nation would meddle so strenuously, and often to ill effect, in his country. In recent months he has become more openly critical of Pakistan and its military leader, General Pervez Musharraf, accusing Musharraf of failing to police his side of the border and allowing Taliban and al-Qaeda fighters to cross into Afghanistan at will, something that U.S. and NATO commanders in the International Security Assistance Force have complained about as well.

Karzai's destination in 1983, Quetta, is a conservative town in Baluchistan, a province of Pakistan's northwest frontier and a deeply traditional part of the country. Baluchistan comprises a vast area that stretches from Afghanistan's southern border to the Arabian Sea. The province lies on what was the northwest frontier of British India and is a keystone in the concept of Pashtunistan, which, if ever realized, would swallow up huge pieces of both Pakistan and Afghanistan. The British, after trying without success to militarily subdue the Pashtuns, or

Pathans, finally granted semiautonomous status to the region, a political designation that continues, de facto, today—Baluchistan is in what Pakistan calls the Tribal Areas, over which Islamabad has only limited authority. In 1893, King Zahir Shah's ancestor Abdur Rahman Shah signed a treaty with the British governor of India, Sir Mortimer Durand. The Durand Line established the boundary between Afghanistan and India, dividing the Pashtuns between the two countries. The line was deeply resented and never considered legal by the Pashtuns, who fought from the beginning to reunite their tribe. Unification never happened, though, and became immeasurably more difficult after the bloody partition of India in 1948 that created a new nation, Pakistan, which inherited all the territory on the Indian side of the Durand Line and wasn't about to cede any of its land to Afghanistan. The treaty that created the Durand Line expired after a century, in 1993, leaving the Afghan-Pakistani frontier in a state of legal limbo that continues today. The border remains in effect on the ground, but it is as porous as ever, which gives fits to the United States and its NATO allies who liberated Afghanistan from the Taliban in 2001. It is widely accepted that the Taliban and al-Qaeda cross the border freely in both directions, while the American forces and NATO troops are bound to respect the line and Pakistan's policing of the tribal areas is ineffectual. Quetta and Peshawar were the breeding ground for the Taliban movement, and the Taliban and al-Qaeda enjoy broad-based support in those areas today.

When Karzai arrived in Quetta in January 1983, he found, not surprisingly, that it was very much like Afghanistan—the same people, the same customs, the same music. "Actually, there was mainly Afghan music in the shops, and I'm sure the same is true today," he said.

The Afghan refugees were very well received by the local people—it must have almost seemed like a reunification of the Pashtuns, although on the Pakistani side of the Durand Line. The acceptance by Pakistan and Iran of millions of Afghan refugees demonstrated broad support for the anti-Soviet jihad, which was heartening to Karzai. He was also pleased to note, after his brief but troubling exposure to Islamic extremism during his journey from Simla, that the extremists remained on the fringes of society in Quetta.

The elder Karzai was head of an office in Professor Mojaddedi's ANLF organization, and Hamid went to work there and lived in a house in Quetta with his father.

Sibghatullah Mojaddedi was a respected Islamic scholar, widely traveled—he had set up Islamic study centers in Oslo and Copenhagen, where he had gone to escape possible arrest or death after Daoud's 1973 coup—and politically moderate. He had been an early opponent of Afghanistan's nascent Communist movements, and had been imprisoned in Kabul for five years, from 1959 to 1964, on trumped-up charges that he had joined in a plot to kill Soviet premier Nikita Khrushchev. He founded the ANLF in 1979 to fight for Afghan liberation and independence.

The ANLF was one of seven major parties that had been formed to resist the Afghan Communist governments and the Soviet occupation of Afghanistan. All had offices in Quetta and in Peshawar, which was a few miles to the east of the legendary Khyber Pass and was much more firmly under the control of the Pakistani government. Young Afghans swarmed into both cities to enlist in the jihad.

The resistance groups ranged in ideology from the poisonously extreme Hezb-i-Islami headed by Gulbuddin Hekmatyar to the moderate ANLF, which attracted traditionalists and royalists like the Karzais. Hekmatyar, whose forces would later reduce much of Kabul to rubble, is said to have earned his stripes as a fanatic Islamist in the 1970s by throwing acid into the faces of unveiled women on the campus of Kabul University, where he was a leader of the shadowy Muslim Brotherhood.

While sharing a common goal of defeating the Soviet Union in Afghanistan, the many resistance groups had no grand coordinated strategy for their struggle. The jihad was fought by individuals, by small groups, by tribes and villages, by provinces. "It was a national struggle, but not a unified or coordinated one," Karzai said. Guerrilla-style military operations were carried out by groups, both large and small, of mujahideen. Operational details such as when and where to attack or how to approach an objective were left to the commanders in the field.

Like America's ill-fated war in Vietnam, the conflict in Afghanistan was, in military terms, asymmetrical—a conventional force on one side, and indigenous guerrillas on the other. The mighty Red Army rolled into Afghanistan in heavy tanks, and its ground forces were supported in the air by MiG and Sukhoi fighter-bombers and the heavily armed and greatly feared Hind helicopters. The mujahideen, like the Vietcong, were lightly armed (with the same Russian-designed Kalashnikov assault rifle the Vietcong had used) and approached their engagements on foot, often crossing high, snowbound mountain passes, shod only in sandals, walking for days or weeks to reach an objective. The Soviet troops did not speak Pashto or Dari and relied on Afghan translators who were often double agents. The mujahideen could take shelter and receive food, water, and intelligence in virtually any village.

At first, not many observers gave the Afghan fighters any chance of defeating the Soviets. I was told of a conversation between an American and an Afghan mujahid in Peshawar one day in the early years of the jihad.

The American, who had just come out of Afghanistan, said that things looked bad, that the Soviets were too strong, that the Afghans couldn't hold out forever. He pointed to the sidewalk and remarked, "I hate to say it, but finally they'll flatten you as flat as this pavement." The Afghan said nothing until they came to a small crack in the sidewalk where weeds had begun sprouting. "Yes," he replied, "the concrete seems permanent, but look at those weeds. Now think about all the ancient cities and fortresses around here. They once seemed permanent, but now they're in ruins, thick with weeds. It's the same with us and the Soviets. In the end, the weeds will win."

The story echoes what a Taliban official was reported to have said after U.S.-assisted forces had driven the Taliban from power: "The Americans have the watches, but we have the time."

"We were always optimistic," Karzai said. "I don't think there was anyone who gave up hope. We all knew that eventually we would win, and drive the invaders from our country."

At the ANLF headquarters in Quetta and Peshawar, the Karzais and other party leaders dealt mostly with the larger picture—the political, diplomatic, and logistical support of the mujahideen. "Day to day we tried to make sure the fighters had the weapons, ammunition, clothing, food, and other supplies and medical care they needed to carry out their operations," said Karzai. As the resistance attracted more and more international attention and presence—and support, in the form of arms and money—the job included engagement and negotiations with governments including Pakistan, Saudi Arabia, the United States, Britain, France, and others. Over time, more and more of this activity would be delegated to Hamid Karzai. The party organizations grew larger and developed sophisticated structures with various departments and committees—military, political, and operational.

The Soviet invasion brought the world to Afghanistan's doorstep for two principal reasons. The first was humanitarian. Refugees were streaming across the country's borders into Pakistan and Iran. Western relief agencies, largely unwelcome in Iran, descended on Pakistan's northwest frontier in great numbers to help Pakistan cope with the sudden and massive influx of refugees and to provide a wide range of services from health care and education to the manufacture of prosthetic devices for war-wounded Afghans, many of whom lost legs to antipersonnel mines planted by Communist forces or the so-called butterfly mines sown by the tens of thousands by Soviet aircraft. The plastic wings of the small mines ensured wide dispersal when dropped from a few thousand feet, and their dull green color allowed them to blend into the terrain, but their size and shape tended to attract children, who lost hands, arms, and sometimes eyes when they picked up the devices.

Most of the humanitarian organizations remained on the Pakistani side of the border, focusing their efforts in Peshawar and Quetta. Médecins Sans Frontières (Doctors without Borders) and two other French medical organizations went inside Afghanistan, its physicians risking their lives to provide medical care for injured mujahideen. One MSF physician, Dr. Laurance Laumonier, walked hundreds of miles and spent many months in the mountains of northern Afghanistan, where she tended to the wounded of Ahmad Shah Massoud's forces as they held off repeated assaults by the Soviets and the Afghan Communist forces.

The other chief motivation for international aid to the Afghans was political. When the Soviets invaded

Afghanistan, the U.S. government reacted immediately. Overnight, Pakistan became a front-line state in the cold war, and its relations with the United States, which had been near the breaking point, suddenly improved. President Jimmy Carter had cut off aid to the Pakistani government of military strongman Zia ul-Haq in April when Zia refused to abandon his ambition to make Pakistan a nuclear state. In November a Pakistani mob attacked the U.S. embassy, burning it down and killing a U.S. Marine. But the Soviet invasion called for U.S.-Pakistani differences to be quickly papered over so that the United States would be able to use Pakistan as a conduit for clandestine aid to the Afghan resistance fighters, in the hope of handing the Soviets their own Vietnam-like defeat.

"I think the rest of the world had a hard time believing that the Afghan people could defeat one of the world's two superpowers," Karzai said, "but gradually we began to hear comparisons of the Soviet occupation of Afghanistan with the American experience in Vietnam. The Soviets were bogged down in a war they could not win and which had no end in sight."

"The Great Game" was the label attached to a nearly century-long struggle between the British Empire and czarist Russia for domination of western Asia. The cold war pitted the U.S.S.R against the United States in the aftermath of World War II. Now, in the 1980s, a frontier of the cold war had become a hot war, the Great Game was in extra innings, and Afghanistan was once again the game's pawn.

3

Defeating a Superpower

H AMID KARZAI had left Afghanistan as a schoolboy, but he arrived in Quetta as a man, a young, educated man ready to join the jihad and get reacquainted with Afghanistan, but at a different level of understanding. "I discovered that jihad was also a school," he said, "one that taught me many things, not the least of which was the revelation that there were concerted efforts by outsiders for control of the jihad. These were the efforts that later brought great suffering to Afghanistan."

"The neighbors" were at work.

The Soviet invasion of Afghanistan had redrawn the political map of Southwest Asia almost overnight. Afghanistan under Soviet rule posed a theoretical threat to the other countries in the region. Historically the U.S.S.R. had longed for warm-water ports that could only be reached through Pakistan or Iran; NATO had blocked any potential routes to the Mediterranean. U.S.-Pakistan relations, at a low ebb after the burning of the U.S. embassy, were quickly patched up. Pakistan's military strongman, Muhammad Zia ul-Haq, saw in the Soviet invasion an opportunity to enlarge his own influence in the region. The canny Zia fully understood the calculus of the cold war and the shifts of America's political coordinates that a Ronald Reagan presidency would bring, since Reagan, committed to bringing down the U.S.S.R., would eventually pour aid into Pakistan. And General Zia would determine how that aid money was spent, and to whom it was directed.

Zia appreciated the threat to his own country posed by the Soviets. He wanted an Afghanistan that was both friendly to Pakistan and hostile to the Soviets. Traditionalist Pashtun Afghans, with their loyalties to the king and their still-smoldering dreams of a united Pashtunistan, were not what he had in mind. He made his alliances with the fundamentalists, and through his powerful ISI, the Inter-Services Intelligence agency, the bulk of the U.S. aid went into the hands of those groups.

Three of the seven major Afghan groups were led by moderates who were fighting the jihad from a purely Afghan perspective. These included the Karzais' employer, Professor Mojaddedi; Pir Syed Ahmad Gailani (*pir* means hereditary saint), the head of the National Islamic Front of Afghanistan (NIFA); and Mohammad Nabi Mohammadi, the head of Harakat-i-Inqilab-i-Islami Afghanistan, the Islamic Revolutionary Forces, who later became vice president of the mujahideen government. Karzai also includes Burhanuddin Rabbani (who later became president of the mujahideen government), the leader of Jamiat-e-Islami, the Islamic Society of Afghanistan, among the moderates, although others differ on this point. Rabbani was one of the founders, along with Gulbuddin Hekmatyar, of the violently radical Muslim Brotherhood in the late 1960s. The leaders and followers of the moderate parties were essentially nationalists and patriots, fighting for Afghan values and traditions. There were fewer political agendas, secret deals, or external alliances among these groups. As a consequence, they were last at the trough when the aid money and clandestine military support were given out.

Three major parties were what Karzai calls "nonmoderates," truly extremist groups, partially influenced and financed by Arabs who wanted to impose a radical Islamic ideology on Afghanistan. There was Hekmatyar's Hezb-i-Islami, or Party of Islam; Yunus Khalis headed another branch of Hezb-i-Islami; and Abdul Rasul Sayyaf led Ittihad-i-Islami, the Islamic Union for the Liberation of Afghanistan. Sayyaf's history is a case study in Islamic extremism—he was also a member of the Muslim Brotherhood, was heavily financed by Saudi Arabia during the jihad, was a close ally of Osama bin Laden, and was named in the 9/11 Commission Report as a mentor to Khalid Sheikh Mohammed, the alleged mastermind of the 9/11 attacks. The report also claims Sayyaf helped to arrange the interview in which Northern Alliance commander Ahmad Shah Massoud was assassinated on September 9, 2001.

"These nonmoderates had the greatest share of the backing of the rest of the world, including the West, and as a result the moderates were completely undermined and marginalized," Karzai said, but while it was true that the fundamentalists were getting most of the Western aid, it was because the West was largely ignorant of the species of viper its aid was nurturing and because the Western nations financing the jihad had surrendered the power of the paymaster to Pakistan. Thus the biggest single recipient of Western aid was the charismatic Hekmatyar, whose fiery Islamist rhetoric stirred the faithful and whose utter lack of scruples allowed him to make deals with the nearest devil and strike viciously at anyone in his path. During the jihad, Hekmatyar regularly attacked rival Afghan groups inside Afghanistan, where he was supposed to be directing his forces against the Soviets, and on Pakistani soil, where he targeted moderate leaders and intellectuals. He was also blamed for the murders of Western journalists inside Afghanistan to prevent rivals such as Ahmad Shah Massoud from getting publicity. Hekmatyar's efforts to destroy prewar Afghanistan continued for years after the Soviets withdrew, and continue to this day—he remains in hiding and is doubtless allied with the Arab-led al-Qaeda movement.

Hamid Karzai's job in Professor Mojaddedi's ANLF was in the Operations Department, whose task it was to supply the mujahideen with weapons and outfit them for their trips inside Afghanistan. The party also helped to take care of the refugees in every way that they were able. In addition, the Indian-educated Karzai organized and taught in a program for the instruction of English to Afghan refugees. "Of all the things I did during those years, that English course was one of my best contributions," Karzai said. "It was a great, great work and many young Afghans who learned English in that program went on to continue their educations, some to a very high level. I remember many of those people, and it gives me great happiness to know that I was able to help them with their educations."

The resistance parties, moderate and nonmoderate, held constant meetings during this time, although they did not create a formal alliance until 1985. Karzai enjoyed good relations with Pir Gailani of NIFA, with Burhanuddin Rabbani of Jamiat, and with Mawlawi Yunus Khalis, the head of his own branch of Hezb-i-Islami. "I had less and less contact with Gulbuddin Hekmatyar and with Abdul Rasul Sayyaf, the leader of Ittihad-i-Islami," Karzai said, noting that since he became president he had met several times with Sayyaf and "he has made a good impression" on Karzai, in spite of Sayyaf's extremist history. "Over the past three years [Sayyaf] has worked steadily to strengthen the Afghan state by supporting the Bonn process and the constitution." He is now a member of parliament.

"We often discussed the differences among us," Karzai said of these interparty discussions. "We moderates argued for a loya jirga, and for the return of the king, but the non-moderates argued against our proposals and, unfortunately, they had the money to back up their arguments." While Mojaddedi, Gailani, and Mohammadi were constantly pushing for a moderate, independent Afghanistan, billions of dollars were being pumped into the radical groups who wanted to "de-Afghanize" the country, as Karzai puts it. That is, they wanted to sweep away centuries of Afghan tradition in order to dominate the Afghan people with their extreme views, and to allow massive amounts of foreign influence in the affairs of the nation. "Deep in our souls, we knew that was a path to failure, and so it turned out to be, and that failure took a terrible toll on the Afghan people," Karzai said.

The moderates were actually fighting two battles: one against the Soviet Union, to force them out of Afghanistan, and the other to try to preserve Afghanistan as they, the moderates, knew it—a country with a stable government headed by a king, and with time-honored traditions, a country that "belonged to the Afghan people." It was a struggle against the conspiracies that were hatched against Afghanistan and the efforts to divide and rule. This conflict grew more intense as the Soviet withdrawal became inevitable, and continued long after the last Soviet tank had crossed back over the Amu Darya, the river that forms part of the border between Afghanistan and what was then the Soviet Union.

But that was still years away.

Five million Afghans fled their homeland during the Soviet occupation. Most of them settled in numerous camps in Pakistan and Iran, and Karzai often visited these camps as an interpreter for foreign fact-finding delegations. He once served as an interpreter for His Highness the Aga Khan, Prince Sadruddin, who was then the United Nations high commissioner for refugees. (The Aga Khan is the spiritual leader of the world's Ismailis, a Shia group that formed in the eleventh century. A number of Ismailis live in northern Pakistan, and a small number of Afghan Hazaras are Ismaili. After the fall of the Taliban and the formation of the new Afghan government, the Aga Khan pledged $75 million to help with Afghan reconstruction.) For some of the refugees, life in the camps was much like their lives in Afghanistan. Some refugee camps took on the appearance of permanent villages, with proper houses, schools, and mosques; indeed, in a few cases nearly the entire population of some Afghan villages had followed their leaders across the border into Pakistan when the Soviets invaded. In such places the lives of the people continued pretty much unchanged. Food, clothing, water, shelter, medical services, and other comforts were provided by the international community. Many nongovernment organizations (NGOs) provided a wide range of assistance and various types of education and training for the refugees. After the Soviet invasion, the U.S.S.R. poured hundreds of millions of dollars in aid into Afghanistan,

while the Western nations ended nearly all aid to the Communist regime and instead shifted their contributions to
the Pakistani side of the border to assist the Afghan
refugees. NGOs set up health clinics, schools, and vocational training centers; the UN's World Food Program
provided thousands of tons of food. But still, despite the
aid, the relative safety of the refugees, and the continuity
of their lifestyle, many Afghans found it extremely difficult
to be refugees, uprooted from their ancestral homes.

Karzai believes that one of the positive aspects to the
refugee situation was that a great deal of assimilation took
place. People from various parts of Afghanistan got to
know each other, which might never have happened oth-
erwise. "For example, some Uzbek people from the north
of Afghanistan came to Quetta, which was a southern
Pashtun area, and established a wonderful Uzbek bazaar,
and we loved having them there," he said. "All through
the camps, there was a sense of sharing—everyone had suffered, and we were all in this together." Another positive
aspect was that Afghans were exposed to the wider world,
which few of them had ever seen before. In Peshawar and
Quetta, they could watch Pakistani television and listen to
BBC Radio broadcasts in Pashto and Farsi, see "Bolly-
wood" movies in cinema houses, or watch pirated Holly-
wood movies on videotape. Also, the refugees were introduced to a variety of Westerners, aid workers from the
United States and Europe, and they could study English
tuition-free. Further, they had access to educational opportunities and health care that they had never previously
enjoyed. One consequence of the long refugee experience
was that many Afghans, once they returned to their homeland, had expectations of similar education and health
services in Afghanistan, services that the Karzai government has been hard-pressed to deliver.

Karzai was not among the legendary warriors of the jihad, such as Ahmad Shah Massoud, Abdul Haq, Jalaluddin Haqani, or Rahim Wardak. In Peshawar, he was known among the Western expats who worked in the various aid groups as the "best-dressed Afghan." His role was more intellectual, as his education and language skills plus his status as a Karzai propelled him more and more into the political and diplomatic arenas, dealing with representatives of other Afghan groups and with Pakistani and foreign government officials. But some degree of participation in jihad as a mujahid was obligatory and essential to his credibility and standing in the resistance movement. So Karzai, especially in the later years of the war, 1987 and 1988, would go inside Afghanistan with large or small groups to carry out military operations against the Soviet forces. "I completely understood how incredibly difficult the military side of things was," he said. The Soviets and their Afghan conscripts had a tremendous advantage in firepower. They controlled the roads with their tanks, they controlled the air with their Hind helicopters and Sukhoi fighter-bombers, and they had heavy artillery. While the mujahideen were receiving clandestine military aid from a variety of countries, much of it funneled through the Pakistanis, most was in the form of small arms that could be carried into Afghanistan on the shoulders of the mujahideen or on the backs of mules, horses, and camels.

This was the way jihad was fought: small groups of fighters, carrying small arms and a few RPG-7s (rocket-propelled grenades) or a mortar, would sneak into Afghanistan, perhaps with a particular target in mind, which may have taken several days to reach. When they arrived at the target—it might have been an Afghan army base or Soviet outpost, or an ambush site on a mountain road—they would stage their attack, inflicting as many casualties as they could, and retrace their route back over the mountains into the sanctuary of Pakistan. At other times, the small guerrilla groups would stay in an area for several days, attacking a variety of targets. Many mujahideen operations were accomplished on foot, by small groups of men making very difficult crossings of the mountains, which were snow-covered for several months of the year. Sometimes the fighters were able to use vehicles, "but only if we traveled at night with our lights off and used riverbeds and camel paths as roads," Karzai said. "I still marvel today at how those Toyotas and Nissans and Mitsubishis were able to cross the terrain that they did."

Away from the few paved roads in Afghanistan, vehicular travel is tortuous and perilous. The roads often appear to be no road at all and cling dangerously to cliff faces and steep hillsides; a moment's inattention can send a vehicle plummeting hundreds of feet. Many are ancient camel routes. Seen from the air, they appear as faint scratches on the brown landscape, as though someone had dragged a stick across the earth. These trails, barely wide enough for a vehicle, are frequently blocked by rockslides that must be removed laboriously by hand before vehicles can proceed. And in the days of jihad, there was the ever-present danger of a Soviet helicopter suddenly swooping over a ridge and attacking a caravan of vehicles, camels, or the army mules that the United States supplied to the mujahideen.

Karzai recalled one particular such trip. The little caravan started in Pakistan and went over high mountain passes. They drove for many hours over very rough ground. "We passed through one valley where we had to drive in a river against the current, and across a desert where it was snowing—if you can imagine snow in a desert!" he said. "I stuck my head out of the window of our vehicle and caught a cold." The group drove through the night, finally stopping at around three o'clock in the morning. "When I awoke several hours later I was astonished at the beauty of my surroundings, there in the high, magnificent mountains of Afghanistan. In the afternoon, the sunshine warmed us and restored me to health—my cold of the night before simply evaporated."

While they were stopped there, one of the men fired his weapon into the side of the mountain, and cold, clear water began to pour out. Someone was carrying a tap—he had been this way before—and he jammed it into the hole, creating a water faucet right there in the mountains.

Depending on the route such a group took, and where the Soviet forces were, these motorized journeys would take twenty hours on a good day and much longer if problems were encountered. Once they reached the desired area, the group might stay for fifteen or twenty days, conducting hit-and-run operations and spending time in the countryside, resting, eating, and meeting with local people. "Because the mujahideen had strong support inside the country, wherever we went people would help us with tea and food, whatever they could spare," said Karzai. The local population would also provide intelligence about the movements of the Communist forces. But there was always the risk that a villager was a spy in the employ of the Communists, so the fighters could never completely relax. "We always tried to avoid detection, of course, and we were constantly worried about walking into ambushes."

One night Karzai went with a group of fighters into the city of Kandahar, familiar territory to him. They arrived in the city well after midnight and were nourished with buttermilk given to them by locals. "I remember that operation partly because of the generosity of those people and partly because I never understood the reason we did it," Karzai recalled. He was carrying RPG-7 rounds, and the group of fighters had walked for five or six hours, arriving in Kandahar at around one in the morning. "And after we had enjoyed the tea and buttermilk, we launched a small attack, which lasted only a couple of minutes, then ran away to go back to our bases." Operations like that were effective in the countryside, he felt, but not in the cities, and they could cost unnecessary casualties for little if any gain. "I still think of that as an example of the occasionally misguided tactics of our movement," said Karzai.

Sometimes the mujahideen captured Afghan Communist soldiers, Afghan men who had joined the Communist army. In Karzai's first encounter with captured Afghan army soldiers, he was shocked by what the prisoners told him. "They felt we, not they, were the traitors to Afghanistan, because we had been living outside of Afghanistan in a foreign country while they had stayed to fight for what they believed was right."

Captured Communist soldiers, whether Soviets or Afghans, tended to have a short life span. At times, a captured Russian might be held as trade bait to negotiate the release of a mujahid commander, but often the guerrillas, on foot deep inside Afghanistan, had no way to deal with prisoners. The policy of Karzai's group, however, was to take prisoners to Pakistan and release them to the International Committee of the Red Cross (ICRC). Karzai recalled taking a group toward Pakistan and stopping in a hut in the freezing cold mountains to have tea. One of the prisoners, an Afghan Communist soldier, came to Karzai and said, "Please don't take me to Pakistan. Kill me here and let me die in my own country." Karzai replied, "Why do you think I would give you to Pakistan? Don't worry, I would never do that." When the group reached Pakistan, they released the captives into the custody of the ICRC, and Karzai asked the ICRC to take the man who had begged to die in his own country back to Afghanistan and release him safely, on the Kabul-to-Kandahar highway. "That man is still alive," Karzai said. "I know because he came to me and told me he remembered that incident and that he now realized that I was the true patriot and he had been wrong to join the Communist forces."

A key military turning point in the war against the Soviets came in 1986 with the arrival of U.S.-made Stinger missiles, which were supplied to the mujahideen clandestinely by the CIA. These powerful shoulder-fired missiles, built by the Raytheon Company, used infrared seeking devices and sophisticated navigation systems. They were light enough to be carried into Afghanistan by the mujahideen. In the hands of a properly trained gunner, they were extremely accurate against the attack helicopters and planes of the Soviets. The CIA delivered hundreds of these weapons to the mujahideen, and the Stingers were credited with bringing down three hundred Soviet aircraft. The knowledge that any given group of mujahideen might be carrying Stingers changed the dynamic of the war by forcing the Soviet aircraft to fly much higher, where they were less effective against fighters on the ground. Putting the missiles into the hands of the mujahideen neutralized the Soviets' absolute airpower advantage, and their mounting losses of aircraft and pilots helped to shorten the war.

"I think the rest of the world had a hard time believing that the Afghan people could defeat one of the world's two superpowers," Karzai said. "But gradually we began to hear comparisons of the Soviet occupation of Afghanistan with the American experience in Vietnam." Similar to what the United States had experienced in Vietnam, the Soviets were bogged down in an insurgency, a war they could not win and that had no end in sight.

The major political turning point was when Mikhail Gorbachev came to power in the Soviet Union and delivered a speech to the Communist Party Congress in which he referred to Afghanistan as the U.S.S.R.'s "bleeding wound."

"When the leader of the Soviet Union began saying things like that, it was apparent that he wanted to get out," Karzai said. "We knew then that a Soviet withdrawal was inevitable. Militarily, they had already lost."

By the late 1980s, the Soviet forces had moved away from the countryside, where they were largely ineffective, and into the cities as a last line of defense. By then they could control only the cities and the major highways. And, most significantly, Karzai said, the Afghan people were against them: "No occupation force can stay in Afghanistan against the will of the Afghan people. None ever has, none ever will. So we knew at that time the Soviets would leave. What we did not predict was the disaster that followed."

Karzai remembered talking to a young American journalist in 1987. "I had just established the information branch of the ANLF and it was perhaps my first serious interview with a journalist. He asked me, 'Will the Soviets withdraw?' And I said yes, they will. By then, we had fought the Soviet Union to a standstill."

And in April 1988, Pakistan and Afghanistan, with the United States and the Soviet Union as guarantors, signed an agreement that called for the Soviets to withdraw all of their troops from Afghanistan by February 1989.

Karzai did not foresee what would come about after the Soviets withdrew, though others apparently did. Back in 1985, he had been sent to France to attend a journalism course offered by the French government for Afghan information officers, which was to be his role in the ANLF. Two people went from each of the seven parties. "I remember walking down a street in Paris with a friend from the Hezb-i-Islami party who was also attending the course," Karzai said. "We were talking about France, and what a great place it was, and as we strolled I was saying to my friend that when the Soviets finally withdrew, Afghanistan would be at peace and we would be like France, progressive and prosperous. My friend disagreed, saying, 'No, there are other forces at work here.'"

The Hezb man told Karzai that after the Soviets withdrew there would be years of fighting among the radical groups for control of Afghanistan. Karzai did not believe him. "Better said, I did not *want* to believe him." Karzai had only been exposed to the fighting in the southern and southwestern areas of Afghanistan, especially in the Kandahar area, his home territory, where the tribes and not the radicals were dominant. He did not yet understand how much influence the extremists were having in other parts of the country.

"And, of course, sadly," he said, "it happened exactly as my friend said it would."

4

Losing the Peace

As the World Withdraws

T HE FOUR-PARTY agreement that led to the withdrawal of the Soviet Union from Afghanistan was negotiated in Geneva between the Communist government of Afghanistan and the government of Pakistan, with the United States and the Soviet Union acting as guarantors. In the sometimes convoluted machinations of international diplomacy, the mujahideen had no standing. Officially, the Afghan Communist government had "invited" the Soviet Union into Afghanistan. Pakistan, which had provided a refuge for the Afghan resistance, was officially the nation aggrieved by the de facto Soviet occupation of its neighbor. The United States, which had given clandestine support to the resistance through Pakistan, and the

U.S.S.R., which had provided military assistance to the regime in Kabul, were "interested parties" and the logical guarantors.

The mujahideen groups were unhappy about not being included in the official agreement, as they felt that they had just defeated one of the world's superpowers. There had been, however, back-channel discussions between the resistance and the Najibullah government, "some secret and some not so secret," according to Hamid Karzai, about the nature of post-Soviet Afghanistan. "There had been informal contacts in Geneva between the resistance and Kabul, and arrangements had also been made for informing the resistance groups about what was going on in the four-party talks."

The Soviet Union agreed to withdraw all of its troops from Afghanistan by February 15, 1989. Another part of the agreement called for what was termed "negative symmetry": the United States and the Soviet Union would not interfere in the affairs of Afghanistan, and would discontinue the supply of weaponry, an arrangement that was honored more in the breach than in reality.

"The factions of the resistance differed in their views on this agreement, and some groups rejected it simply on the grounds that the mujahideen had been excluded," said Karzai. But overall, the mood among the resistance parties was upbeat. The weeds had defeated the sidewalk, and the Soviet Union was going to withdraw. The seven-party alliance began intense preparations for the post-Soviet period, but the alliance was already divided along the lines that had formed during the years of struggle against the Soviet invasion. There was a group of three moderate parties, and another of four more extreme ones. The moderate group consisted of Professor Mojaddedi's ANLF, Harakat, and NIFA. The group of four included Jamiat-i-Islami, Ittihad-i-Islami, Hezb-i-Islami (Hekmatyar), and Hezb-i-Islami (Khalis). There was, however, some cross-over between the groups. "For example, Rabbani and Khalis were quite close to the three-party alliance and participated in many of the meetings," said Karzai.

Hamid Karzai's role in the ANLF had been expanding, thanks to his family background, education, language ability, and natural charm. The party relied on him more and more as its liaison with the Western nations, and he developed close relationships with U.S. officials and other Western diplomats. Among those relationships were undoubtedly close contacts with the CIA, and the alliances Karzai made during jihad would leave him in an ideal position when years later Afghanistan would need a new leader in the post-Taliban era.

The ANLF was the most devotedly royalist party, and its leadership maintained constant contact with King Zahir Shah in Italy. Hamid Karzai was the party's emissary. "In 1988, I began making regular trips to Italy, once or twice a year, to visit His Majesty," said Karzai, who unfailingly refers to the king in this manner. "These visits would increase in frequency later, in the years of the Taliban." Karzai said he found the king fully engaged with the issues of Afghanistan, always optimistic, and "a most perceptive Afghan." There in Italy the king would tell Karzai exactly the same things that he would hear from tribal chiefs or religious leaders inside Afghanistan. "And His Majesty would always ask, as my father did, 'Do you have the United States with you?' And when I said, 'Yes, we have the Americans with us,' he would say, 'Good. Now we can do it.'" Meaning, Zahir Shah believed the resistance could bring an end to the succession of Communist governments in Afghanistan and restore the independence and sovereignty of the Afghan people if—and perhaps *only* if—the United States stood behind the effort and supported the jihad with money and matériel. "He was always very realistic, very pragmatic," Karzai said. "One of the great joys and achievements of my own life is that I was able to go to Rome in April of 2002 and accompany His Majesty King Zahir Shah back to his beloved Afghanistan, to the palace where he had ruled, after an absence of nearly thirty years."

As the Soviet withdrawal was under way, at the urging of the United States and Pakistan (and Saudi Arabia, which had an interest in promoting a fundamentalist Sunni government in Afghanistan as another check on Shia Iran) some three hundred Afghan tribal leaders gathered in Islamabad to establish a government-in-exile. "Some senior tribal chiefs refused to attend because the meeting was not held on Afghan soil and because, they said, it was organized by outsiders," Karzai said. "Nevertheless, voting took place and Professor Mojaddedi was elected president and Professor Sayyaf was elected prime minister."

No country was willing to give the Afghan Interim Government (AIG) official recognition as the legitimate government of Afghanistan in exile. "But that didn't really matter to us," Karzai said, "because we saw the formation of the AIG as a step forward. It bonded the resistance together in a way that it had not been before." Any feelings of unity were fleeting, however. Gulbuddin Hekmatyar, who had been elected foreign minister, soon split with the AIG, and Professor Rabbani was named in his place. Hekmatyar, whose fighters were rated as only mediocre by military analysts during the jihad, went on to become one of the most destructive and divisive warlords of the post-Soviet and post-Taliban periods.

When the Soviet Union pulled out, it left behind a puppet government headed by President Muhammad Najibullah, who had succeeded Babrak Karmal in 1986. Najibullah was a Pashtun, but had been a Communist since his student days. After the Soviets invaded Afghanistan in 1979, they installed him as the head of KHAD, the Afghan equivalent of the Soviet KGB. In that post, he became one of the most hated and feared individuals in Afghanistan, earning a reputation for brutality.

The feeling among the resistance groups, Western governments, and the Peshawar-based Western aid community was that the mujahideen would march into Kabul in triumph, and the Najibullah government would simply vanish like chaff in the wind. "We in the resistance thought that Najibullah's government would crumble and collapse," said Karzai. "We were dead wrong about that." The Soviet-trained and -equipped Afghan Communist army turned out to be a much better organized and much tougher military force than the resistance had thought. "We discovered that through a very painful lesson when we launched an attack on the city of Jalalabad in 1990, soon after the creation of the AIG," said Karzai. Jalalabad, nearly equidistant from Peshawar and Kabul, is the Afghan city closest to the Khyber Pass, the major road link between Pakistan and Afghanistan, and is the eastern gateway to Kabul. "We were badly beaten there in a battle that was a disaster for the mujahideen," said Karzai. "The countryside and the villages may have been outside of their control, but the major cities stayed in the hands of the Communist government, and would remain so until the eventual surrender." The Najibullah government would hang on for three years without direct Soviet military support.

The mujahideen had other surprises in store. Not only was the post-Soviet Communist government stronger than anticipated, but Afghanistan itself was not the same place the refugees had fled during the war years. "The Afghan psyche had changed during the Soviet occupation," said Karzai. "We in the resistance were now outsiders, and those Afghans who had chosen to remain in Afghanistan throughout those years were insiders."

Also, many mujahideen who had fought for years against the Soviets now wanted nothing more than to lay down their arms, return to their homes, and get back to tilling their fields. They felt the resistance had accomplished what it set out to do, which was to drive out the Soviet Union, and for them the war was over, the mission accomplished. Karzai discovered this mind-set shortly after the Soviet withdrawal. "I was in a village south of the city of Kandahar and I came across a man who had been a very good mujahid," he recalled. "His name was Shinkalai Malang. *Malang* means a type of religious person, someone who is sort of reclusive and solitary. The man's full name means 'the malang with the blue dress,' and he always wore a blue outfit. So I asked him what he was doing, and he said that after the Soviets left he had not wanted to fight against Afghans, so he stopped fighting and went back to farming."

There were many fighters who felt that way and laid down their arms, men who had been considered to be among the best mujahideen, according to Karzai. But the great majority of the resistance continued to fight against the Communist government from their bases in Pakistan, and the great majority of the refugees living in Pakistan, Iran, and elsewhere did not return to Afghanistan. In essence, the Soviet pullout had changed very little. "We associated all the brutality of the years of the Soviet occupation with the Najibullah government, and felt we had to continue the jihad," said Karzai. And throughout the 1990s the majority of the refugees stayed put until after the

Taliban were defeated in 2001, thus avoiding all the years of terrible conflict inside Afghanistan. It was not until the Taliban were driven from Kabul and an interim government was formed under Hamid Karzai that the refugees began returning in great numbers. Many had not seen their homes in twenty years, and while they had been in exile they had given birth to a whole new generation of Afghans, many of whom would not set foot in their native land until they were in their teens and twenties, and who would bring a new set of values and expectations to the country.

During the three years' struggle against the Najibullah government, other difficulties emerged. Even before the Soviet withdrawal the resistance groups had begun to battle for dominance. After the pullout, that fighting began to intensify as the various groups maneuvered for power, so that by the time Najibullah finally handed power over to the mujahideen in 1992, the resistance was in disarray. Hekmatyar's forces, supported by U.S. aid funneled through Pakistan's ISI and by a wealthy Saudi named Osama bin Laden, were engaged in open warfare with the legendary northern commander Ahmad Shah Massoud, who had also received substantial covert backing from the United States. These two dominant forces were maneuvering to be in a position to capture Kabul when Najibullah eventually surrendered. Najibullah's regime was also in turmoil, as factions of his government began to read the writing on the wall and fight each other for survival. The powerful Tajik warlord Abdul Rashid Dostum, Najibullah's key ally in the north, defected, along with his militia, in February 1992 and took sides with Massoud. For Najibullah, Dostum's defection spelled the end of his reign. A new round of UN-sponsored negotiations in Geneva resulted in an agreement for Najibullah to hand over power, not to the mujahideen parties per se but to an "impartial administration," through a step-by-step process. "That's when the Najibullah regime really began to crack, and we in the resistance began to prepare for the change-over," said Karzai.

As the Najibullah government began to come apart and collapse in on itself, government garrisons switched sides and towns began to fall to the resistance. But things were already going wrong, and the path to Kabul for the mujahideen was marked by much more bloodshed and atrocity.

Among the first towns to fall was Tirin Kot, in Oruzgan Province. Karzai recalled, "As we were heading toward Tirin Kot, one of the commanders called me and urged me to hurry because the town was about to fall. I told him to go on ahead, and I reached the town three days later. When I did, I was sickened by what I saw." There had been a slaughter, and many dead bodies lay around. Some were Communist soldiers, but others were civilians, and they were all Afghans. "And I thought, why were these people killed?" Karzai said. "And who killed them? I have been looking for the answers to those questions ever since and have still not found them. Now I believe those killings, those atrocities, should have been a sign for us, but we were not clever enough to see it at the time." The terrorist tactics were a new phenomenon, no doubt inspired by a brutal ideology that was injected into the struggle through men like Hekmatyar, whose thirst for power knew no limits and whose extreme fundamentalism was encouraged and supported by his Saudi backers and the ISI.

As the mujahideen advanced and took more towns, said Karzai, the signs of outside influence and of a cold-bloodedness alien to even the famously fierce Afghans became more and more troubling. "When Kabul was finally handed over to us, the mujahideen, two years later, the same killing went on," Karzai said, "but in a much more open, blatant manner as the mujahideen factions battled each other. Then we truly saw the complete crumbling of the Afghan state."

Meanwhile, another state was crumbling. Within two years of the Soviet Union's withdrawal from Afghanistan, the mighty Communist superpower collapsed. The Berlin Wall fell, the Iron Curtain disintegrated, the map of eastern Europe was redrawn with the emergence of newly independent nations. The cold war was over and the West had won. This world-shaking series of events, the earthquake of the U.S.S.R.'s collapse and its many aftershocks, had clear and unhappy consequences for Afghanistan. The Western world's interest in Hamid Karzai's homeland had been predicated on one principle: stopping the advance of the Soviets in South Asia and, as a bonus, embarrassing the Red Army as the United States had been embarrassed in Vietnam by its inability to defeat an insurgency. With the Soviet Union gone, that interest evaporated overnight.

By April 1992, military power in the resistance had been consolidated into two main forces, those of Ahmad Shah Massoud and his northern fighters—recently augmented by Dostum's militia—and the forces of Gulbuddin Hekmatyar, advancing from the south. The Afghan capital was caught in the jaws of these two armies, but in this case the jaws were working against each other as well as against Najibullah's remaining forces. Massoud made the first and preemptive strike, moving his forces into the city, meeting only token opposition from the remnants of the Afghan army, seizing the airport and most of the major buildings in the capital. Hekmatyar had been caught asleep at the switch, and his forces held only a fragment of the city.

Karzai recalls the event vividly. "I was with the first group of mujahideen to enter Kabul in 1992, after the

Najibullah government had agreed to hand over power. I traveled to Kabul with Professor Mojaddedi, who was now president, and it was an incredible experience." Karzai had not seen the city of Kabul since 1978, when he left following the violent coup against Daoud Khan. In April, as Massoud's forces were massing at the city's eastern entrance, Karzai was in Peshawar, where the government-in-exile had been meeting, trying unsuccessfully to persuade Massoud and Hekmatyar to join forces. Hekmatyar refused. Karzai remembers the arrival of the mujahideen in Kabul as a triumphant and somewhat orderly event. "We traveled in a convoy, hundreds of us, representing all the resistance parties," he said, though Hekmatyar did not accompany this convoy, which was led by Massoud on a tank. "We drove from Peshawar to Jalalabad to Kabul. The night before we entered the city we stayed in a place near Pol-i-Charkhi, near the military academy. I shared a room with my friend General Noruz, the military chief of staff of the Afghan Interim Government, a professional soldier of the finest order. It was a very cold night." In the morning, the Afghan army was there to escort the mujahideen into the city. "I was surprised to see how polished and professional a military force they were," Karzai said of his first close-up look at the Soviet-trained force the mujahideen had been battling for years. "Their uniforms were neat, their weapons and vehicles were polished, and they behaved like disciplined soldiers. The army leaders went into a small room with President Mojaddedi and discussed the terms of surrender, and then we got into our vehicles and headed for Kabul."

The residents of the city, who had been unnerved by the sounds of battle as the resistance armies had closed in on the capital, were understandably wary of the conquerers. "As we drove into the city, I could see that there was some fear in the population," Karzai said. "As we passed the big Soviet-built apartment blocks of the neighborhood of Microrayon the curtains on the apartment windows were drawn shut, and I could see the people inside peeking out through little openings in the curtains, watching us pass by."

The leaders of the entourage were temporarily housed in a mansion that later became the embassy of the United Arab Emirates. Karzai looked at his former hometown with a sense of wonder. "Kabul was still intact then, the last time it would be so," he said. In all the years of war against the Soviets and later against Najibullah's government, the capital had been spared. It was still the clean and orderly place Karzai remembered from his youth. The city's great buildings, including all the ministries and mosques and the magnificent Darlaman Palace, which had been built for King Amanullah in the 1920s, were standing unscathed. Virtually all of them would be destroyed in the years of fighting that followed.

"I was thrilled to be there, but even on this occasion, which should have been a joyful celebration, there was a foreshadowing of the tragedies to follow," Karzai said. The triumphant mujahideen fired thousands of rounds of rifle fire into the air in celebration, and the falling bullets killed dozens of innocent Afghans, including the brother of Karzai's roommate of the night before, General Noruz.

There was some street fighting as the last of Najibullah's army resisted the takeover, but most of the gunfire was celebratory. But the mixture of thousands of fighters from Massoud's and Hekmatyar's factions was volatile and would soon explode into the beginnings of yet another Afghan war.

The new government had been formed in discussions among the resistance groups in Peshawar, under the guidelines set forth in the transfer-of-power agreement.

Professor Mojaddedi would serve as president for two months, then Professor Rabbani would assume the presidency for four months, and would preside along with a supreme council made up of mujahideen leaders. After that a grand loya jirga would convene, the permanent government would be chosen, and the nation would move ahead in that way. "Of course, nothing worked out as planned," said Karzai. "What happened was that when the mujahideen took power, the factional fighting became institutionalized warfare."

In fact, within hours of the official transfer of power the battles began between Massoud and Hekmatyar, whose forces began pounding away at each other and reducing Kabul to rubble, building by building and block by block.

The seeds for this destructive warfare had been sown well before the handover, Karzai believes, when some of the mujahideen leaders and "outside interests" came to Kabul on their own for discussions with the Najibullah government. "There were many behind-the-scenes intrigues as each faction, each power, each country tried to grab a piece of the capital or a piece of the country that they would dominate."

The day after the mujahideen's victorious arrival in Kabul, Karzai went to the Ministry of Foreign Affairs to take up his new position as deputy minister. "But from that day forward, things proceeded badly for Afghanistan. Miserably!" he said. Any semblance of national unity was quickly laid to ruin. The military and its weaponry were divided, and the parties would write their names on the guns and tanks and aircraft that they took. Within two or three years, what had been in Karzai's estimation a "very good Afghan air force," consisting of some four hundred fixed-wing aircraft and more than a hundred helicopters, simply vanished, along with hundreds of well-trained pilots. Kabul was split among three or four parties, and other Afghan cities were similarly fragmented. In Kandahar, Karzai's ancestral home, tribal loyalties trumped party affiliations as the city was divided among three or four tribes. The only major place that remained in the hands of one man was the western province of Herat, which borders on Iran, and its capital city, also called Herat. "Under the strong leadership of Ismail Khan, Herat remained peaceful and began to prosper," said Karzai, who would later bring Khan to Kabul. Elsewhere, including in the city, life became a daily horror as the fighting factions began what Karzai called a "systematic" destruction of Afghanistan's buildings, property, heritage, and institutions, and the mass destruction of human life itself. "I say 'systematic' because I believe it was the aim of some of these factions to destroy the very fabric of Afghan life and to render the country helpless. Our victory over the Soviets turned to misery and defeat."

Professor Mojaddedi was in office only for his allotted two months, and then he left and the Leadership Council of the interim government elected Rabbani president, as per the arrangement that had been worked out earlier in the Afghan Interim Government in Peshawar. But, according to Karzai, "The real troubles began then." Hekmatyar rejected the process and began what would be a three-year barrage of rocket fire into the Afghan capital, which would kill thousands of people and destroy countless buildings. Massoud's forces shelled Hekmatyar's positions in response. Other groups joined the fight. "Some days we could not even leave our homes, and sometimes our houses themselves were damaged by rocket fire," said Karzai. "My own house was hit twice. We tried to keep on functioning as a government and remain impartial, but it was impossible."

The interim government itself was by then hopelessly divided. Karzai recalled that one day a man came to his office in the Ministry of Foreign Affairs and told him that two Pakistanis had been arrested because they had been seen walking with two men from the prime minister's office. "And I said, 'How can we possibly explain such a thing to the outside world, or to the Afghan people, that the president's men could arrest someone for walking with the prime minister's men, or vice versa?' It was a world turned on its head, completely outside of any standards of normalcy that anyone would recognize."

In his role as deputy foreign minister, Karzai appealed constantly to the UN and to his old friends in the West for help, but none was forthcoming. It was abundantly clear now that Afghanistan had been written off by the West after the fall of the U.S.S.R. "This was when we really saw the abandonment of Afghanistan by the West," said Karzai. "We had not noticed any diminution of Western involvement after the Soviet pullout in 1989, and even the weapons had kept coming in despite the 'negative symmetry' provision in the Geneva accords. As long as we were based in Peshawar, we had the full participation of the Western diplomatic community. But the moment the mujahideen took power in Kabul, the West left."

The United States had in fact left months before, when the CIA's fund for Afghan operations had expired. The British embassy, which had remained open in Kabul throughout the Soviet occupation and the Afghan Communist government, also pulled out. "I told them very strongly not to do it, but they did," Karzai said. The American embassy had left Afghanistan years before, and had never returned, though the American government had supported the resistance practically throughout the fight against the Soviet Union. Now, in the spring of 1992,

Western disengagement was complete. Afghanistan was relegated to the status of a nonentity. "And that was the reason behind the subsequent misery that we all suffered—we, the Afghans, for so many years, and then the Americans and the rest of the world on 9/11," Karzai said.

Without the involvement of the West, Afghanistan was vulnerable to other influences, to ideologies hostile to the West, but most in the West failed to recognize the threat. Osama bin Laden, the wealthy Saudi who would later become the world's most wanted criminal for orchestrating attacks on the West, had been quietly operating in the shadows of jihad for years and had been seen in and around Peshawar in the 1980s. He raised funds in Saudi Arabia to support the extremist factions headed by Hekmatyar and Sayyaf and recruited young Saudis to fight in Afghanistan. Around 1988 he founded the group known as al-Qaeda, which, like the Mafia's cosa nostra ("our thing"), simply means "the base." Bin Laden's vocal opposition to the Saudi royal family finally got him expelled from the kingdom in 1991, and he focused all of his attention on supporting the radical Islamist movements in Afghanistan and in Africa, where he bought a home in Sudan from which he directed attacks on U.S. targets in Yemen and Africa.

As Karzai recalled it, the mujahideen period was a time of great intervention by other powers. "Not help—intervention. The country was suddenly open to all of the neighbors, with all of their designs on Afghanistan," he said. "If they wanted to destroy, they could destroy. If they wanted to play one party against another, they could. If they wanted to kill, they killed. Some good people were trying to speak up for Afghanistan, but they were voices in a wilderness of savagery." Afghanistan had lost its voice, and by its exit from the Afghan stage the West, according to Karzai, had a direct hand in undermining Afghan sovereignty.

Karzai finally left Kabul in 1994 because it had become impossible to stay there. Though he had what he described as very good relations with President Rabbani, and with Abdul Rasul Sayyaf, the foreign minister, conditions in the capital continued to deteriorate. In spite of the near chaos outside, Karzai had reported for work every day at the ministry, "except for those days when the rocket attacks were so intense we could not leave our houses," he said. Then one day an Afghan man who was a stranger to him came to his office and said that President Rabbani wanted to see him. "I had my doubts, because this was not the usual way I would have been called to meet with the president, but I said, Okay, let's go." The stranger took Karzai to a building where he knew very well that President Rabanni would not meet anyone, and led him upstairs to what appeared to be an interrogation or investigation office. "We sat down, and another man, also a stranger to me, arrived and began to ask questions, such as Who was on the side of the ANLF? Whose sides were various people taking? These were very inappropriate questions for these men, whom I did not know, to ask of me." Karzai's life may have been in danger—he was in an unsecured location with men he did not know in a murderously violent city—but just as he was about to respond and demand an explanation, a rocket hit the building above their heads, sending dust and debris and broken glass showering down on them. Karzai fled the building and returned to the ministry, washed off the blood and debris, then found the foreign minister and told him about the incident. "He was shocked that such a thing could happen, and it was an indication to us both that the situation was out of control. Then I told him that I was leaving." Karzai hired a vehicle and drove out of Kabul, to Peshawar and then on to Quetta. President Rabbani issued a very strong statement about the incident, condemning the people who had questioned Karzai and calling them the enemies of the Afghan state—but by that time his words carried little weight.

The stories from that period tell of suffering, of destruction, of the selling out of the country, of the misery and poverty of the Afghan people. They are stories of how Afghans who had returned fled back into Pakistan and other countries. "They are stories of a determined effort, an effort organized from outside, to kill the spirit of Afghanistan," said Karzai.

So it was that when the Taliban appeared on the scene, the majority of the Afghan people—including Hamid Karzai—were drawn to them.

5

The Rise of
the Taliban

T HE TALIBAN first arose from the ranks of former mujahideen groups, and they were called Taliban because they came from religious schools—the word *talib* means a religious scholar. Many of the religious schools, called madrassas, were on Pakistani soil, and many of their students were young Afghan boys whose families had fled to Pakistan and became refugees during the Soviet occupation of Afghanistan. The madrassas taught a very harsh, puritanical brand of Islam unlike anything prewar Afghans had known. Most Afghans had subscribed to the Hanafi school of Sunni Islam, which espouses the most tolerant interpretation of the Holy Koran; the madrassas taught Wahabism, brought to Pakistan in large measure by the Saudis, who were attempting to influence the religious and political nature of post-Soviet Afghanistan. By enrolling young Afghans and limiting their knowledge to this restrictive theology, the madrassas were creating legions of young zealots who would march under the white banner of the Taliban, cloaked in an aura of religious purity.

The ongoing civil war in Afghanistan had by 1994 reduced the country to a fractured, lawless state, a patchwork of regional warlords and criminal gangs. Afghans were in desperate need of peace, order, and stability, and in the Taliban they thought they saw a savior. Only a loose affiliation of groups in the early 1990s, the Taliban began to cohere as a force and gain a reputation for righteousness after an incident in the spring of 1994. As Karzai tells it, a warlord in Kandahar kidnapped two girls from a rival group, and the girls were gang-raped at the warlord's base. A small group of Taliban attacked the warlord's base, freed the girls, and hanged him. Word of the dramatic rescue spread rapidly. The Pakistanis took notice as well and supplied the Taliban with weapons, vehicles, and military advisers.

Pakistan was greatly concerned with the trade route to Central Asia, which crossed southern Afghanistan. The route was being controlled by Hekmatyar's forces, which insisted that Pakistani trucks not cross into Afghanistan but that cargoes be loaded onto Afghan trucks at the border. Even then, the route was perilous and the trucks were often hijacked by armed gangs. After the Taliban captured the border town of Spin Boldak from Hekmatyar's forces, Pakistan enlisted them to free a hijacked convoy, which they did. That same week the Taliban captured Kandahar, and their march to Kabul began.

"The people of Kandahar, virtually everyone there, voluntarily surrendered to the Taliban because of all the killing, looting, and destruction that was still taking place at that time as the mujahideen factions continued to battle one another," said Karzai. Some mujahideen groups fought briefly against the Taliban but were quickly defeated because the Taliban had gained widespread popular support and the mujahideen did not fight wholeheartedly. "We had high hopes for this movement," said Karzai. "We hoped the Taliban would bring peace and restore Afghanistan to the hands of the Afghan people. President Rabbani supported them; so did I, so did other Afghan groups."

The Taliban began to move north toward Kabul and west toward Herat, which was controlled by Ismail Khan, whose forces resisted for several weeks before the Taliban finally prevailed in September 1995. Ismail Khan took refuge in Iran. The Taliban reached the outskirts of Kabul the same year, defeating and disarming Hekmatyar's fighters along the way, but were stymied by Ahmad Shah Massoud's forces, which continued to hold the capital. Finally in late August 1996, the Taliban, heavily supplied by Pakistan and the Saudis, captured Jalalabad, the eastern gateway to the capital, and seized Kabul itself a month later. The ousted Communist president Najibullah, who had been given sanctuary in a United Nations compound in 1992, was dragged from the compound and hanged near the presidential palace. It took the Taliban another two years and heavy losses to capture Dostum's northern stronghold of Mazar-i-Sharif, but the losses were soon made up by new recruits from the Pakistani madrassas and new shipments of weapons and vehicles. By the autumn of 1998, the Taliban controlled 90 percent of Afghanistan's territory. The remaining 10 percent, the mountainous north, was held by Massoud and a coalition of Tajiks, Uzbeks, Turkmen, and Hazaras that united under the flag of the Northern Alliance.

The Taliban never did assert their control over the northern areas, though they imposed a harsh rule on the rest of Afghanistan. Virtually sealing off the country from the outside, they enforced a brand of Islam that horrified the world.

"The Afghan people accepted the Taliban at first because they brought a sense of law and order where there had been lawlessness, killing, and destruction," Karzai said. "Wherever the Taliban took over there would be peace. There was also oppression, serious oppression." They took the country backward, banning many widely accepted forms of modernity.

All forms of entertainment were banned, including kite-flying. "They would force people to destroy their radios and TVs; they banned all forms of music." Men were forbidden to trim their beards. The five daily prayers, which Afghans were accustomed to performing at whatever place they happened to be at prayer time, now had to be performed in a mosque. But it was the Taliban's treatment of women that drew the condemnation of much of the outside world.

No woman could go out in public without being accompanied by a male relative—a troubling burden on women whose husbands and other men in the family had been killed in the long years of fighting. Even when accompanied, a woman was required to wear a burka, the all-concealing shroud that forces the wearer to see the world through a fine grillwork. Women were forbidden to work or go to school, though the Taliban promised to reopen girls' schools when they had rid the country of impure elements. "And," said Karzai, "they enforced their rules with beatings, maimings, and executions." Most shocking to the West were the beatings in the streets for the tiniest infractions, and the gruesome spectacles of beheadings and stonings in stadiums, which the public was required to attend and watch in silence.

The Taliban also enforced a principle of nonnegotiation and no compromise. "After the Taliban had established control in Kabul, they refused to share any power with the mujahideen groups who had helped them get there," said Karzai, "and many disaffected mujahideen then began to turn against the Taliban regime."

Karzai became disaffected with the movement early on. "The first time I realized something was wrong with the Taliban movement was quite soon after they began their march toward Kabul in 1994." As noted, Karzai had resigned from the now dysfunctional mujahideen government, left Kabul, and returned to Quetta, where Professor Mojaddedi's base was still located. A member of the Taliban, a mullah Karzai had known from the years of the fight against the Soviets, came to see him there. "This mullah had come out of Afghanistan and he had brought a sick man to see me in hopes that I could arrange treatment for him in Germany or somewhere in the West. When we had finished our discussion about the ailing man, we began to talk about Afghanistan. 'Mr. Karzai,' he said, 'this Taliban movement is going forward. But I would like to tell you something.' There was a table in front of us, and the mullah spread open his right hand as wide as he could, with his fingers straight and extended, and laid his hand flat on the table. 'Foreigners would shed the blood of thousands of Afghans to take this much of our land,' he said, indicating his spread-open hand. 'They would kill thousands of our people for it. They would have no mercy.' That was only in the third month or so of the Taliban movement, and already I had gotten my first warning that all was not right."

The next warning Karzai received was from another

mullah, Mullah Yar Muhammad. One day he came to Karzai's office in Quetta and told him, "There are some people whom we don't know in this movement now. They just suddenly appeared in our country. Who are they? We don't know them, and yet they are better equipped, they have better weapons. What is going on? Why are we Afghans so poor, when these strangers are doing so well?"

Mysteries arose during the Taliban's advance on Kabul—like the sudden surrender of places without any visible Afghan involvement. "There were times when the top Taliban leaders, the commanders, were in Kandahar and places far away would fall. Who did it?" said Karzai. "These mysteries continued. And so I began to understand that the Taliban movement had been infiltrated."

There was another sign of trouble within the movement: by 1995, the Afghan Taliban were no longer keeping in contact with Karzai. "I learned that they were discouraged from contacting me or coming to our house in Quetta, where my father and I continued to work for Professor Mojaddedi's organization and continued to try to engage the Western nations to help Afghanistan." The Taliban leadership had begun to see Karzai as an opponent, and they were correct. By the middle of 1995, he knew there was something seriously wrong, that the Taliban were losing their Afghan character and the movement was being taken over. By whom? "One day a helicopter pilot came to see me, a man I had not known before, to say that he was now working for the Taliban," said Karzai. "He came to the house several times for discussions, and in the third or fourth meeting he told me about a mission he had flown for the Taliban. He was told to transport a tall, bearded Arab man, along with a foreign military officer, to Kandahar from somewhere in the provinces to the east. This Arab man was carrying two suitcases full of money, the pilot told me, and he was taken to see Mullah Omar and Mullah Rabbani at the Taliban headquarters."

After hearing the pilot's tale, Karzai became aware that a lot of people from the Arab countries, as well as other foreigners, had moved into the area around Kandahar International Airport.

More and more stories like this began to emerge as people in the Taliban movement whom Karzai knew, Afghan mujahideen from the time of the jihad, also began to tell him of troubles inside Afghanistan. Then he learned that the Taliban had placed him off-limits. One man told him that a "foreign intelligence officer" in Kandahar had told him to stay away from Karzai. "Later, when U.S. forces were looking for this man for questioning, we arranged his surrender, but he ran away to Pakistan, where he was arrested by the Pakistanis and turned over to the Americans, who took him to Guantánamo. By running away he had made himself a criminal suspect." Another time, after the Taliban had taken Kabul and were fighting against the forces of Ahmad Shah Massoud in the north, a young Talib came to Quetta and hung around Karzai's house for several days waiting to see him. "Finally someone said, 'This guy has been waiting for a week. Find time to see him.' So I arranged to see the young man after dinner, and when we had finished the meal I called him to my meeting room, upstairs in the house where we worked. 'Who are you?' I asked." He gave Karzai his name and said he was from Oruzgan Province, in central Afghanistan. He told Karzai he had been in Parwan Province, which is north of Kabul, and that he had witnessed a strange thing. "He said he had been part of a group of around a hundred fifty Taliban who had been told to move into the Ghorband district of Parwan to take control of the area. But when they approached a district village they discovered that another force had been there earlier and had killed a lot of people. There were bodies lying around. 'And we wondered who had done this,' he told me. 'We were the ones who were supposed to have attacked this place.'" The next morning, the young fighter told Karzai, they saw a convoy of four or five big SUVs with blacked-out windows drive past them. "After they had passed by," the Talib told Karzai, "our commander brought us together and said, 'It's a mystery who these people are who got here before we did. Who are we fighting for? I thought we were fighting for Afghanistan, for good government, but there is somebody else.'" The commander went off by himself to think things over, and then called his group together again. "I do not believe in this war anymore," he told his fighters. "It is not ours. It is not an Afghan thing. Those of you who want to leave may leave. There will be no penalty for that."

The young Talib told Karzai that he then left his group and walked to his village, where he told the story to his father. And the father told the son, "Go to Quetta and tell Karzai." And that's what the young man did; then he left and Karzai never saw him again.

"That incident confirmed two things for me," Karzai said. "One, it was true that foreign hands were destroying Afghanistan; and two, I had become a main center of opposition to the Taliban in the southwest. I had not known the young Talib, or his father, and yet the father had sent him straightaway to me."

According to Karzai, there was an obvious, visible effort on the part of the Taliban to disgrace Afghanistan, to cause ethnic hatred, to insult Afghan society and rob it of its guts, its courage. "They were trying to strip the Afghan people of their identity, to dehumanize and deculturize them. For example, to beat a woman in the streets, or to beat a husband in front of his wife because the wife was wearing the wrong color shoes, humiliated people." Karzai was told of this tactic by a United Nations worker from Bangladesh, who was part of the UN mission that was then still in Afghanistan. "He told me he had witnessed the same humiliation in Bangladesh and recognized it immediately as a systematic effort to take the Afghans' character from them, to kill their spirit and replace it with nothing but religious extremism. Islam? The Taliban were not practicing Islam. Rather, they were the tool for defaming Islam. They were out to destroy Afghanistan and Islam together. Whatever they did was against Islam: humiliating women is not Islam, depriving children of education is not Islam, destroying lives is against Islam, and selling their country is against Islam." The Taliban had become the agent of a foreign power bent on emptying Afghanistan of thousands of years of history and culture, Karzai believed, and the Afghan people began to recognize this, especially after the systematic killings of Afghan leaders, including Karzai's own father and the great commander Abdul Haq, and the destruction of the Buddhas of Bamiyan. The two colossal figures of Buddha, one of them 175 feet tall, had been carved into the sandstone cliffs of Bamiyan eighteen hundred years ago, before Islam came to Afghanistan. They were a historical treasure, but in April 2001 the Taliban destroyed them with dynamite and artillery, reducing them to rubble despite worldwide protests. "The Afghan people saw this was wrong, but by then they were powerless to resist," said Karzai. In Hazara-dominated Bamiyan, the Taliban were despised. Hazaras had fought for the Northern Alliance in the battle for Mazar-i-Sharif and were systematically slaughtered by the Taliban in reprisal. In Bamiyan today, residents claim the destruction of the Buddhas was overseen by Pakistani military advisers.

Although Karzai and his father were not inside Afghanistan, they had excellent access to information through their past associations with mujahideen who were now in the Taliban movement. This information kept coming despite the warnings to have no contact with the Karzais. As more and more stories came to them about the steady reduction in Afghan authority in the movement, Karzai began to consider organizing resistance against the Taliban. "But before it reached that stage we tried to talk with them," said Karzai. "We sent a very senior delegation to Kandahar in early 1995 to see Mullah Omar, but he refused to see us and sent his number two, Mullah Rabbani, to meet with our delegation." Karzai's delegation proposed that the Taliban accept help from Afghan experts—economists, engineers, technocrats—to help run the country they were conquering, but these proposals were rejected.

When the Taliban took Kabul in 1996, they appointed Hamid Karzai their ambassador to the UN, but he rejected this appointment for obvious reasons: "I would not have been representing Afghanistan but someone else," he said.

In 1998, the foreign minister of the Taliban, who was still a good friend of Karzai's, was asked to meet with the U.S. chargé d'affaires. As the Taliban official later related the incident to Karzai, the American chargé said the United States had information that there were terrorist training bases in Khost Province, which is in southeastern Afghanistan and borders on Pakistan. The foreign minister said, "Well, if you're asking me, I don't know about such things. We don't have any bases there." The chargé said, "But we have evidence." And the minister said, "If you have evidence of these things, then you know where these bases originated, and you know where their supply lines are, and you must also know who established these bases, and where the real centers of this activity are. So in that case you are talking to the wrong person." Within three months of this conversation the minister was removed from his post, according to Karzai. The matter of the terrorist training bases was not in the Taliban's hands.

By the end of 1995, Karzai had begun to openly oppose the Taliban, and in 1996 he began to actively organize against them. It began with discussions among the leadership of the ANLF and the other moderate Afghans based in Quetta and spread out from there. On Karzai's visits to the various foreign embassies in Islamabad, he spoke out against the Taliban and warned the Western governments of the danger signs in the movement. But on one such embassy visit, a Western diplomat told him, "You are speaking so openly against the Taliban. Watch it, man! They'll smash you." As Karzai tells it, the diplomat said it as though he was speaking for the Taliban—as if he did not like that Karzai was opposing them. "But the more I learned about what was happening in Afghanistan, the harder I worked against the Taliban." He organized meetings in Islamabad, followed by an intra-Afghan dialogue with meetings of Afghan groups in Istanbul. This process culminated in a big meeting in Frankfurt in 1998, followed by a meeting of forty senior Afghans in Rome. "By then the anti-Taliban movement had grown enormously, and everyone was taking part—President Rabbani, the ANLF, Ahmad Shah Massoud, all of us," said Karzai. "What came out of those dialogues was total Afghan resolve, and a call for a loya jirga." The anti-Taliban coalition issued statements, which were picked up by the world press. "We also delivered these statements to the Taliban, and invited them to participate in the loya jirga, but all such approaches were rejected."

Karzai constantly engaged the international community

during this period and would meet in Islamabad on almost a weekly basis with the U.S., British, German, and Italian embassies. He made regular trips to Rome to report to King Zahir Shah, who proposed a program for unseating the Taliban regime that included a loya jirga. Karzai also traveled to Washington, D.C., a number of times, addressed the Senate Foreign Relations Committee, attended many other House and Senate committee meetings, and met with State Department officials. "My rounds didn't gain me much more than political support," he said. "There was no real backing for a military operation inside Afghanistan. Perhaps Afghanistan was not considered that important, perhaps the misery of the Afghans and the killing of Afghans did not matter to those countries. We were a poor country, with little to offer the world in terms of trade." And, Karzai said, the Western governments were looking at the situation in Afghanistan from a purely Western perspective. "I now understand that while these countries may have supported us in principle, they did not see that within our hearts and souls we had the power to remove the Taliban. They were measuring strength only in terms of guns and tanks. They could not hear the heartbeat of a strong nation that had the will, but not yet the means, to end the horror in Afghanistan."

Along with Afghan tribal leaders and disaffected Taliban, journalists would also come to Karzai in Quetta, and he would do interviews for the radio—BBC, Voice of America, Radio Liberty. His voice was having an impact that he was not aware of at the time, but the BBC's Dari and Pashto services had long been staples of the information diet of Afghans, and even though the Taliban forbade listening to such programs, many Afghans tuned in surreptitiously on hidden radios. "In one interview I called on the Taliban to get rid of the foreigners in the country," said Karzai. "I said the problem is not with you, the Afghans, it's the foreign Taliban who have taken over the country. That broadcast had a powerful impact. After that the Afghans in the Taliban came under a lot of pressure because they were no longer trusted by the outsiders who were controlling the movement."

The Taliban and their backers were alarmed by the Karzais' activities, and Hamid had become a highly visible and very vocal opponent. They first tried to placate him, to win him over. Once they sent some tribal chiefs to him to ask, "What is it you want? Come and join us. Do you want to be foreign minister? We'll appoint you." In response, Karzai wrote a letter to Mullah Omar telling him that the Afghan people had hoped for a lot from him but he had delivered instead misery and despair, a lack of education for Afghan children, a loss of independence for the country, and internal fighting. "I told him the only way out for him was to call a loya jirga for Afghans to settle these issues—there was no other way. Other than that, he was doomed." Mullah Omar responded that he could agree to some things Karzai demanded, but not to a loya jirga.

The Taliban also threatened Karzai. It was because of his dissident activities and outspoken opposition to the Taliban that they killed his father in 1999. "Maybe they came after me," he said. "Maybe they missed me and killed my father instead because they could not find me. I had no people around me, protecting me." Hamid and his father had discussed the possibility of assassination many times, and the elder Karzai would say, "They won't hurt me, because I am an old man and they know that you are doing the whole job. Protect yourself!" Even the day before his father was killed, Karzai recalled, "he came to my house in Quetta, just across the street from his, and some of our men walked with him, surrounding him, and he said, 'What are you boys doing? They're not going to hurt me. Stay around him!' Meaning, stay around me." But the next day the senior Karzai was shot to death.

It was Karzai's father's wish that he be buried in his native village. In carrying out this wish, Hamid relied on the basic respect of his fellow Afghans. "I took his body from Quetta into Afghanistan, to Kandahar," he said. "Hundreds and hundreds of Afghans joined the procession and the Taliban made no move to interfere."

After the assassination of his father, the U.S. ambassador to Pakistan said to Karzai, "We think you should leave. They will kill you, too." Karzai said to him, "No, I'm going to stay. Rather than asking me to leave, get me support!" Subsequently the Taliban did try to kill him, too, but by then he was surrounded by a stout defense. "And God kept us," he said.

In June 2000, Karzai sent a "night letter," a clandestinely distributed pamphlet, into Afghanistan, to Kandahar, urging people to resist the Taliban, to end this regime that, the letter said, had sold out the country to foreign rule and caused such trouble among the people. "We sent a fifteen-year-old boy on a bicycle around Kandahar late in the night, distributing twelve hundred copies of the letter," said Karzai. "The Taliban panicked. They moved massive forces into the city, blocked the roads, and took up positions all through the city."

After the Taliban were driven from Afghanistan in 2001, they started using night letters themselves, scattering them throughout Afghan villages and warning the residents not to cooperate with the NATO and coalition forces or they would face beatings, torture, and summary execution.

Through all this Karzai continued to talk to anyone who would listen, and he continued to work against the Taliban on a minute-to-minute basis, calling people who were inside Afghanistan, receiving them in Quetta, getting information from them and telling them what was going on outside Afghanistan, and trying to boost their morale. "The reason we were ready when the world finally came to our aid was because of this massive backdrop of support we had organized beforehand," Karzai said.

The story told by the helicopter pilot who had come to him some months before, about a tall, bearded Arab with suitcases full of money, had alerted Karzai to the influence of another foreign element, other than Pakistan, at work in Afghanistan. The tall Arab was, of course, Osama bin Laden. Although he had insinuated himself into Afghan affairs during the jihad days in the 1980s, he would have had no contact with Professor Mojaddedi's moderate ANLF, preferring to use his money and ideology to win influence with the extreme Islamist groups, especially Hekmatyar's and Sayyaf's.

"Perhaps everyone, including ourselves, bears responsibility for allowing and condoning the arrival of people like him," said Karzai. "But the West and the radical, extremist Muslims worked together, and no one can absolve the West of responsibility for what came of that cooperation."

Afghanistan's recent past, which saw the promotion of religious extremism and a massive disrespect for the nation, brought great misery to the Afghan people. Bin Laden was allowed to operate openly, to set up his training camps in Kandahar and other parts of the country, and so it was that international terrorism had at its disposal the infrastructure of a state with a military, with functioning airports and even some planes, and with massive amounts of weapons.

At the same time in 1998 when the Taliban's foreign minister was telling the American chargé d'affaires that he knew nothing of the terrorist training camps in Khost, the U.S. embassies in Dar es Salaam and Nairobi, in East Africa, were bombed by al-Qaeda. The August 7 blasts, simultaneous car-bomb explosions, killed more than 250 people and injured thousands more. The United States held bin Laden directly responsible for the attacks. On August 20, President Clinton sent cruise missiles into Afghanistan, aimed at bin Laden's training camps in Khost, and into Sudan, attacking a facility that U.S. intelligence had identified, perhaps erroneously, as a chemical weapons plant owned by bin Laden.

Karzai asks today, "Should President Clinton have done more at the time? Yes, but not only he—the whole world should have done more. If the world had done more, the Twin Towers would be standing today." That lesson, powerful and recent though it was, is already being ignored. Trouble is back, and Afghanistan is again in need of rescue.

Images of Afghanistan Today

The Arg is the presidential palace in Kabul. The sprawling compound holds
numerous structures, including the president's office and residence,
the king's residence, a mosque, and quarters for the palace guards.

A view across the valley to the sandstone cliffs where the famous Buddhas of Bamiyan stood for over a thousand years. The empty niche visible here held the larger of the two Buddhas, which stood around 175 feet high. A smaller niche is out of frame to the right. The Buddhas were reduced to rubble by the Taliban in 2001.

Bamiyan is the home of the Hazaras, a Shiite minority whose ancestors originated in Mongolia. Two laborers head home at the end of the day.

A close-up of the niche where the large Buddha stood. Tunnels, carved into the cliffs by the monks who inhabited the valley before the arrival of Islam, gave access to the upper reaches of the Buddha. The opening near the top of the niche once allowed people to step out onto the Buddha's head.

Outside Habibia High School in Kabul, where President Hamid Karzai attended school, students' bicycles offer evidence of the Afghans' eagerness to return to school after the fall of the Taliban. The school was heavily damaged during the years of civil strife in Afghanistan and was in the process of being rebuilt with aid from India.

A sidewalk vendor fries *boulani*, tasty pancakes
filled with leeks and potatoes.

An Afghan Boy Scout proudly wears his uniform at Habibia High School. He had recently attended a Scout Jamboree.

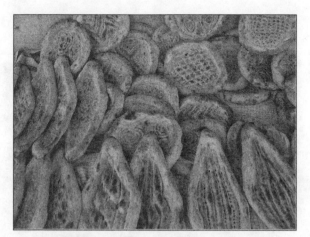

The delicious flat bread called nan is baked fresh
all day at tiny neighborhood bakeries.

Carpet sellers outside their shop on Kabul's famous Chicken Street,
a longtime magnet for tourists, where carpets, Afghan jewelry, and
other souvenirs are offered for sale in dozens of small shops.

A broom maker and his son push their wheelbarrow full of brooms through the streets of Kabul, offering them for sale. The brooms have short handles; most sweeping is done in a squatting position.

In 2004 many Kabul women still wore the burka. Although
Afghan women continue to dress very modestly, the number
who wear the burka is steadily diminishing.

Kabul's newfound affluence, fueled by an influx of foreign aid
workers and a construction boom in the capital, is evident in the
consumer goods offered for sale in the shops. Computers, cell
phones, and these Chinese motorcycles are very popular.

With the ouster of the Taliban and the influx of foreign aid money, Kabul
became a boomtown, and its population more than doubled in a short time.
Newcomers found what space they could, often on the rocky hillsides
surrounding Kabul, and put up mudbrick houses.

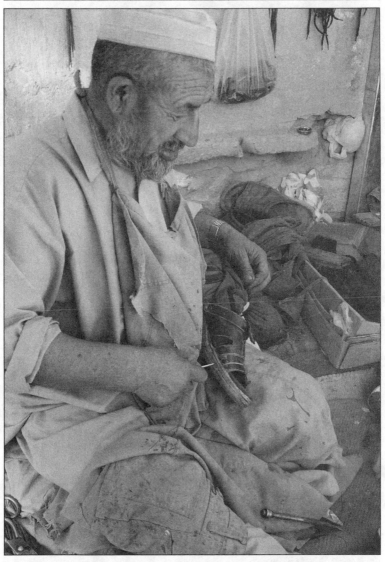

Many goods and services are offered right on the sidewalk rather than in shops. Here a cobbler plies his trade in the Shar-e-now section of Kabul.

The debris of war is piled high in a Kabul junkyard, awaiting recycling.

Three young Afghan boys take a break at a sidewalk machine shop in Kabul.

After the fall of the Taliban, Kabul blossomed.
The bazaars are full of goods and buyers.

The neat, colorful displays of grains and spices attract
shoppers in Kabul's old bazaars.

The Bird Bazaar, a narrow, twisting pathway in one of the oldest sections of Kabul, offers a variety of birds from parakeets to pigeons, falcons, and even owls. Afghans are fond of birds as pets.

Many parts of the city of Kabul suffered heavy damage
during the years of warfare, but the commerce continues
in the ruins and the city is rebuilding itself rapidly.

Afghanistan is famous throughout the region for its sweet melons.

A street vendor sells bananas grown in Afghanistan.

The long, oddly shaped tool this man carries is a mattress fluffer. The device is inserted into a cotton-filled mattress and is said to set up vibrations that fluff up the stuffing and restore the comfort of the mattress.

During the reconstruction of Habibia High School, students
attended classes in 2004 in tents donated by Unicef.
The reconstruction was completed in 2005.

The village of Istalif, an hour's drive north of Kabul, has long been a
popular place for family outings. President Karzai's family came
here often to escape the bustle of the city and have picnics.

At around noon, smoke rises from hundreds of charcoal grills
all over Kabul as lamb, beef, and chicken kebabs are
prepared for lunch at small restaurants.

Istalif is famous for its distinctive pottery. More than fifty Istalif
families are engaged in the trade.

One of Istalif's best-known potters, Abdul Wakil, in his shop.

Kabul's construction boom has created jobs for many Afghan men. The construction methods are labor intensive, whether the structure is a private home or a high-rise office building.

Many families whose homes do not have running water rely on these public water pumps, which are found in many parts of the city.

In a makeshift outdoor classroom, his chalkboard propped against an exterior wall, an Afghan schoolmaster teaches math.

A picture of a Kabul man, taken outside a shrine where he had been paying homage.

A carpet seller on Chicken Street.

A firewood seller weighing wood in a Kabul bazaar. Wood and charcoal are widely used for cooking fuel and sometimes for household heat. Almost no homes in Afghanistan have heating systems, and Afghans rely on wood fires or kerosene stoves to get them through the winter months.

Afghanistan is famous for the quality of its pomegranates, which comprise one of the country's major fruit crops. The pomegranate has gained somewhat in popularity in the West recently because of its antioxidant properties.

(This and facing page) Afghan refugees playing buzkashi in Peshawar, 1987. One of the riders has possession of the carcass of a calf and is trying to return it to a chalk circle; if he manages this, he will win a prize. Riders on his team are trying to clear the way for him, while riders on the opposing team are trying to take the carcass from him. Most of the riders are northern ethnic Afghans—Tajiks, Uzbeks, and Turkmen. As in a polo match, riders bring several horses to a buzkashi and switch to a fresh horse between rounds.

A number of street photographers using old-style box cameras operate in Kabul and elsewhere in Afghanistan, meeting the demands for instant passport photos. The pictures are developed on the spot.

A Bedford truck is stopped for inspection on the Pakistani side of the Pakistan-Afghan border at the legendary Khyber Pass, the eastern gateway to Afghanistan, in 1987. The Afghan checkpoint, about a mile inside Afghanistan, was manned at the time by Soviet forces. There are very few places north of the Khyber Pass where a vehicle can cross the Hindu Kush mountains.

6

September 11, 2001

The War on Terror Begins in Afghanistan

O N SEPTEMBER 9, 2001, two Arabs posing as journalists set up a video camera at the mountain stronghold of Ahmad Shah Massoud and prepared for an interview with the legendary commander, dubbed the Lion of Panjshir, after the beautiful mountain valley where he was born and that he had successfully defended for so long. Massoud had survived the long years of warfare against the Soviet Union, which tried time and again to blast him off the face of the earth with aerial bombardment, tanks, and cannons. He and his army of northern Tajiks, Uzbeks, and Turkmen had continually frustrated the Soviets and managed to hold the northern mountains throughout the war.

When the Communist government finally fell in 1992, Massoud became defense minister of the ill-fated mujahideen government. When the Taliban took Kabul in 1996, he retreated to the mountains and held off repeated Taliban assaults, just as he had against the Soviets, whose field officers expressed grudging admiration for him as the mujahideen's most brilliant military commander. The Russians later supported him in the fight against the Taliban. Handsome and charismatic, intelligent and soulful—a warrior poet—Massoud rarely left the mountains, but freely granted interviews to journalists willing to make the trek to the Panjshir and had become an international folk hero during the conflict. His opposition to the Taliban went beyond his military efforts; he made repeated appeals to the United States and other Western countries to help remove the Taliban and their Arab allies from Afghanistan. This made him the enemy not only of the Taliban and their leader, Mullah Mohammed Omar, but of the shadowy Osama bin Laden, whose reputation as a terrorist mastermind had been enlarged by the bombings of the U.S. embassies in Africa in 1998.

Massoud took a seat in front of the camera the Arabs had set up. Beside him was his longtime friend Masood Khalili, the ambassador to India for Massoud's organization, the United Islamic Front for the Salvation of Afghanistan. Khalili was fluent in several languages, including English, which one of the Arabs spoke as well.

One of the Arabs turned on the video camera, which instantly exploded. A powerful bomb had been hidden in it, and Massoud's security had neglected to check it. Massoud was gravely wounded. One of the Arabs died instantly, and the other was shot by Massoud's bodyguards as he tried to run. Masood Khalili was also seriously injured, as was documentary filmmaker Faheem Dashty, who had been working on a film about Massoud.

Massoud was flown by helicopter to a hospital in neigh-boring Tajikistan, where his supporters continued to insist that the commander had survived the blast, but other observers said he was almost certainly dead at the scene of the bombing.

The assassination of Massoud was linked to al-Qaeda, but whether it was planned as a precursor to the attacks of 9/11 is unclear. It does make sense that bin Laden would have wanted Massoud out of the way before 9/11, leaving his forces in disarray, knowing that the United States would almost certainly come after the Taliban following the attacks in America. Hamid Karzai was not sure if there was a connection. "Whether his assassination was linked somehow to the attacks of 9/11, or whether the timing was purely coincidental, we may never know. What we do know is that a great Afghan warrior was lost."

In life, Massoud was a hero, but in death his stature approached sainthood. He was named Afghanistan's national hero, and his image is ubiquitous there—on postage stamps, on shop walls, in homes, and in full color, several stories high, on Kabul's airport terminal, beside a slightly smaller image of President Karzai. Had Massoud lived to see his Northern Alliance drive the Taliban from Kabul, he would have been a serious contender for the presidency.

On September 11, 2001, Karzai was in Islamabad, making the rounds of the embassies. He had heard about the attack on Massoud, but it was not clear at the time that the Lion of Panjshir had died. Karzai had met with Massoud in the months before 9/11 to discuss the ongo-ing campaign against the Taliban and had been moving closer to a decision to escalate his movement from vocal opposition to armed insurgency. After his day's discus-sions in Islamabad, Karzai went for a walk before dinner. It was the end of the day in Islamabad, but just the beginning of that unforgettable day in the United States.

"My cell phone rang," said Karzai. "I heard the voice of my brother telling me that a plane had just struck one of the towers of the World Trade Center in New York City. As soon as I heard that, I somehow knew immediately that it had not been a mistake. When the second plane struck minutes later I knew for certain this was an act of terrorism."

After the call from his brother, Karzai canceled the next day's embassy meetings. "After all," he said, "there would be no point in reminding them of what I had been telling them for the past six years." Karzai's warnings to the West about the dangerous extremist movement that had found a safe haven in Afghanistan under the Taliban had proved correct, in a most horrifying way. He prepared to return to Quetta, knowing that the time for talking was over. Now it was time to go inside Afghanistan and remove the Taliban.

In the days after Karzai's return to Quetta, hundreds of people arrived in the town from all over, convinced that now something would happen. Karzai had become the recognized leader of the anti-Taliban movement, and Afghans looked to him for direction. Under the Taliban, Afghanistan had become a pariah state, recognized only by Pakistan, Saudi Arabia, and the Arab Emirates. Now that the United States had been attacked by terrorists who had almost certainly been trained in Afghanistan and sent on their suicide missions by Osama bin Laden, Afghans anticipated a major response by the Americans and their allied countries. Perhaps Afghanistan was going to be returned to the Afghans.

"There were large crowds around our house, and more kept coming," Karzai said. "Over the next few days I quietly made my preparations to leave for Afghanistan. I had been ready for some time." Back in March, he had met with Ismail Khan, the powerful Herat commander who had taken refuge from the Taliban in Iran, to coordinate with him. Earlier he had gone to see Massoud in the north. What's more, Pakistan had refused to renew Karzai's visa, probably due to his anti-Taliban activities. "There was nothing left for me to do," he said. "My only options were either to give up or to move into Afghanistan, rally support, and fight."

The day before Karzai left Quetta he instructed one of his brothers to get money for him. He told his brother that he was moving inside. "He was shocked, and pleaded with me to change my mind, but I said, 'No, I'm going.'" The next day at around five in the afternoon Karzai told his wife that he was going to the border to visit the family of someone who had died, to offer his condolences. He asked her to pack a change of clothing and his toothbrush and toothpaste. "She said, 'Why will you need those things? You can go and come right back.' I said, 'Well, I don't think so. If I don't come back in two days, or if I don't call you in two days, then just forget about me.'" Karzai's wife was shocked, but before she could say anything else he closed the door and ran off. "I didn't want to give anyone the chance to stop me," he said.

During the days Karzai spent in Quetta before heading inside Afghanistan, he held meetings with a variety of people, including unspecified American officials, who promised to bolster his efforts once he was inside. He had no way of knowing how soon or how extensively the Americans would become militarily involved in Afghanistan. He had promises of military support but was not sure if that meant air support, troops on the ground, or just weapons and ammunition. As things turned out, he had all of this and more.

In the hours and days in the immediate aftermath of 9/11, the Bush administration's focus fell on Afghanistan and Osama bin Laden. Washington made a number of demands on Pakistan, including the use of Pakistani air bases and territory as staging areas for U.S. military operations, something Pakistani president Pervez Musharraf found politically impossible to agree to. After all, Pakistan recognized the Taliban as the legitimate government of Afghanistan, and its intelligence service, the ISI, was deeply involved with the movement.

The Bush administration also demanded that the Taliban arrest Osama bin Laden and turn him over to the United States. The Taliban representatives in Islamabad replied that they had asked bin Laden to leave, but would take no action against him.

In Afghanistan, bin Laden's terrorist training camps emptied immediately after 9/11, as he and his cohorts fled to mountain caves in anticipation of a U.S. attack, leaving no firm targets for American bombers. U.S. military planners also realized that Kabul offered few bombing targets that would cripple the Taliban, as much of the country's infrastructure had been destroyed during the civil war. The best option, they felt, would be to insert commando teams inside Afghanistan to seek out and destroy terrorist hiding places, and to rally the Northern Alliance, now led by Ahmad Shah Massoud's chief military commander, Muhammad Fahim, to attack the Taliban in Kabul and elsewhere, calling in U.S. air support where practical. U.S. emissaries began talks with Northern Alliance leaders, with Pashtun leaders including Hamid Karzai and famed commander Abdul Haq, and even with King Zahir Shah in Rome. The king said he was willing to serve as a standard for Afghans to rally around, though he insisted he would never retake the throne. The United States was also building a coalition that included Britain as a military partner.

The growing fear that a U.S. attack was imminent

threw the Taliban into disarray. There were reports that Taliban soldiers were ready to defect en masse to the Northern Alliance. Mullah Omar slipped out of Kandahar, where he maintained his headquarters as the de facto head of Taliban-ruled Afghanistan, and went into hiding in the mountains. It was into this cauldron of fear, uncertainty, and shifting loyalties that Hamid Karzai plunged to rally his countrymen.

After leaving his house in Quetta, Karzai went to an area near the Pakistan-Afghanistan border and spent the night at the home of a friend. Very early the next morning he continued on to the home of another friend and took breakfast there. Then he met up with three other men, members of his anti-Taliban movement. "We got on motorbikes they had procured, tied turbans around our heads, and rode toward the border on the main highway. It was quiet at that hour and there was not much traffic on the road. Also, there were not many Pakistani police or Taliban guarding the border and we were able to cross into Afghanistan unchallenged." With the expectation of U.S. bombing hanging heavy in the air, a few men on motorbikes didn't attract much notice. When the little group reached Kandahar airport there was a large crowd of Taliban members checking cars and trucks that had come from Pakistan or were headed there. "One of the men with me asked, 'What should we do?'" said Karzai, who replied, "'Let's just go on by. If they stop us, they stop us. If they don't, we move forward.' It worked. The Taliban were occupied with checking the big trucks and didn't give us a second glance. We just moved on. God was with us."

The men continued on to a village that was part of Kandahar Province. It was very quiet. No one was around. They went to the house of a cousin of Karzai's, but his door was locked and no one answered their knocking. Finally a friend turned up and led the men to his house, where he looked after them very well, giving them "a wonderful dinner and a place to sleep," said Karzai. After all, this was the region where Karzai grew up and where many of his relatives and friends lived, and his family was held in high esteem. Now, when he needed their help, they gave it, but not without apprehension. In the morning, their host came to him and said, "This is a very heavy task you are undertaking. Go back. Go back to Quetta. Don't get yourself killed." Karzai thanked him but said no. With the friend's help he and his companions left that house at midday and moved on to another cousin's house. The cousin gave them lunch, but he was so frightened to have the men in his house he wouldn't even let his two-year-old daughter come into the guest room where they were. That night, the U.S. bombing began.

American planes flying from aircraft carriers in the Indian Ocean and even from bases in the United States began hitting a variety of targets throughout Afghanistan. American and British cruise missiles were sent streaking toward Taliban military bases and other suspected command posts, terrorist training camps, and weapons depots. North of Kabul, the soldiers of the Northern Alliance moved to within striking distance of the capital.

The bombs struck a Kandahar depot where the Taliban had stored a large supply of rockets, and rockets began exploding and landing all over the city. "We looked out and saw a lot of people running in the streets, trying to get away from the explosions," said Karzai. "We had no place to go so we just stayed there and hoped that no rockets would fall on us."

In the morning, Karzai's group was joined by another contingent of men from the anti-Taliban movement who had been sent earlier to Oruzgan, north of Kandahar. The group discussed whether they should stay in Kandahar or go to Tirin Kot, the capital of Oruzgan Province, about ninety miles north of Kandahar. "We decided to go north, and a taxi was brought, driven by one of our men, and we headed for Tirit Kot," said Karzai. "We drove for hours, and at around eight in the evening we came to a place where there was a strong Taliban force, and where a curfew was in effect—no one was allowed to pass after eight p.m." A Taliban sentry stopped the men and searched the car. He found the one thing that could have gotten the group into serious trouble: a satellite telephone.

What was left of Afghanistan's meager telephone system after the Soviets pulled out was destroyed during the civil war. Mujahideen commanders had long been accustomed to communicating with handheld radios to coordinate their operations during the jihad. Cell phones, which would become a near-universal accessory in Afghanistan after the fall of the Taliban, were forbidden. Satellite telephones were virtually the only means of long-distance communication.

"What is this?" the sentry asked, holding up the telephone. "Just a box," one of Karzai's men told him. "What do you mean, just a box?" the Talib demanded. He knew it was not just a box. But he was an Afghan Talib, and Karzai sensed that he had "a strong Afghan sentiment." Plus, with the onset of the U.S. bombing, many Taliban were uncertain which side to be on. Karzai did not want to be recognized, so another of the group went up a little hill to where the Taliban commanders were, and managed to negotiate the group's passage. "All right, go," the commanders said.

"And we went, driving on as far as the taxi could take us, to a river, where we got out," said Karzai. "We waded across the river and walked on, and at around eleven at night we arrived on the outskirts of Tirin Kot at the house of a friend, where we spent the night. Then the real stuff began."

The following day the group left the friend's house around sunset and walked for three hours under cover of the Afghan night from one side of Tirin Kot to the other, to the house of a conservative mullah whom Karzai had known for many years and whose brother was a judge in a Taliban court in Oruzgan Province. Karzai had sent the mullah a message asking him to call some senior tribal chiefs of the province to a meeting, and when he and his men arrived at the mullah's house, the chiefs were waiting. "At around nine p.m. I held my first anti-Taliban meeting inside Afghanistan," said Karzai. "We sat down together—the mullah, me, two companions, and four tribal chiefs."

Before Karzai spoke, one of the chiefs said to him, "We know why you are here. Do you have the United States with you?" Karzai said yes, because even before 9/11 he had been in contact with not only the Americans but with the British, the French, the Italians, and others and had enlisted promises of support. He had received messages from Washington and Rome, and some U.S. officials had visited him in Quetta before he went into Afghanistan. "What I did not know was whether they would come, or just send weapons and supplies," Karzai said. The mullah then said, "You have a satellite telephone. Call the Americans and tell them to come and bomb the Taliban command center in Tirin Kot."

Karzai said no, he could not do that. "I could not in good conscience call the Americans and tell them to bomb my people, my country," he said. "So, you are such a patriot that you cannot do this?" said the mullah. Karzai told him yes. "Well," the mullah said, "in that case you don't want to win. You want to be a loser."

"What do you mean?" Karzai responded, somewhat indignantly. The mullah said, "The population is fully with you. We will defend you to our deaths. But these are cruel people we are dealing with, and they have full backing from outside the country. They will have no mercy on us. They will bomb us; they will send rockets into our homes and send the flesh of our women and children into the trees. Is this what you want?" Karzai said no, of course that was not what he wanted. The mullah said, "We cannot win without the Americans. If you can't tell them to bomb, then at least ask them to drop weapons for us." Karzai agreed to that.

Karzai stayed in the mullah's house for several days, and during that time the mullah's brother, the Taliban judge, came to the house for tea every afternoon. He said to Karzai, "You will never win. But I will not report you." However, the Taliban were well aware of Karzai's presence in Afghanistan, and with their situation in deep peril and growing more precarious by the day, they were willing to seek Karzai's counsel.

"After about ten days I returned to the house where I had spent my first night in Oruzgan Province and there I received some senior Taliban delegations," Karzai said. "They told me that if I had the United States with me I would win, but if not, they said, 'Don't even try. Don't damage yourself, your history, or the people of this area.'"

It was obvious to the Taliban that many Afghans now saw Karzai as their leader, the one who would lift the draconian rule of the Taliban from the Afghan people. One night a message came to Karzai that Mullah Omar had called the governor of Oruzgan Province to say that Karzai was in the area, and why didn't the governor's forces take him? And the governor had said, "I don't have the forces." Mullah Omar replied, "What do you mean, you don't have the forces? Karzai has only ten people with him." The governor said, "It's the people; they are on his side. We have tried to reach him twice and have been stopped by the villagers, who warned him we were coming." Mullah Omar said that he would arrange something from Kandahar, and two days later he sent a force of more than a thousand men to capture or kill Hamid Karzai. Again, the people warned him in time for him to make his escape.

"The Taliban force decided to move against us the same night they arrived," said Karzai, "but the people of the area kept us informed and told us of the Talibans' plans." He and his men left that place and walked for two hours to another house, where they spent the night with a tribal elder whose two sons were Taliban commanders; they were also in the house but took no action against Karzai. "Early the next morning we left, heading for the mountains north of Tirin Kot, where we would be out of the reach of the Taliban and could request a weapons drop. We walked for eight hours through a beautiful valley. At the other end we were met by a senior clergyman who led us to a house where we spent the next two nights and where some local tribal chiefs came to meet with us." There, Karzai began to look for a suitable site for a weapons drop.

He needed to find a place away from the villages so that if fighting started there would be no danger to civilians, and away from the Taliban and their pickup trucks so that when the weapons were dropped the Taliban wouldn't get to them first. Using his satellite phone, he called the U.S. embassy in Islamabad to tell them of his plan, and then he headed for the mountains. His group had now grown to about fifty men.

"We started walking at around eight in the evening, and at one thirty in the morning we reached a mountain peak—not the highest peak in that area, but still quite high and very, very cold," Karzai said. "I think that was the coldest night of my life." He was not dressed properly for the mountains, wearing only lightweight summer clothing; even in mid-October the Afghan lowlands were very warm, but once the men gained elevation the air rapidly turned cold. "The climb had made me very warm, and by the time we stopped I was perspiring heavily," said Karzai. "We all lay down for a brief rest, and when we woke up after only twenty or thirty minutes we were all shivering uncontrollably." Karzai hugged his knees to his chest but could not stop shivering. The men collected what wood they could find and made a fire, but not even that warmed them up. So they started to move again, and by nine thirty in the morning they had reached a valley surrounded by magnificent mountains and discovered a family living there in what seemed to them a no-man's-land. "We asked the man for some tea, and he made up huge kettles of tea over a fire," said Karzai. "He had only six cups, so we handed them around until everyone had drunk some hot tea. Meanwhile the man cooked up some pumpkins for us to eat." Karzai and his men stayed there for three days to rest, and the farmer fed them as well as he could, but he was not prepared to feed fifty men day after day. So Karzai sent some men to walk to the nearest village to buy supplies in the bazaar. But the supplies never reached the group. The Taliban had blocked the mountain trails.

Karzai knew that he had to act before the Taliban caught up with him. He used the satellite phone to call the U.S. embassy to ask for an airdrop of weapons.

"Where are you?" they wanted to know. Karzai said, "Well, we're somewhere in Oruzgan." That's when he learned about the superiority of U.S. technology. The Americans asked him in what direction he had come from

Tirin Kot, and he told them approximately which way the group had walked and how far. The Americans told him to make a square of fires, a hundred meters apart, that night, and to call them again the next day.

They gathered wood and made the fires as the Americans had asked. During the night they heard no planes flying over, but the next day Karzai called the Americans again, and they said, "We saw your fires. We know where you are. Make the same fires again tomorrow night and we will make the supply drop at eight o'clock." Again the men made the fires, but the planes did not come. "I called and asked what had happened," said Karzai, "and they replied that the planes were coming from Germany and couldn't reach us in time, but they would do it the next day."

The next night they again made the fires and waited. Eight o'clock came and went. Karzai waited. He was very tired, and at around midnight started to fall asleep. Then at 1:30 a.m. someone shouted, "Planes!"

"I couldn't see the planes, because they were flying without lights, but we could hear them, and when the parachutes opened we could see them drifting down to earth." Two or three landed in the drop zone, but the others were off the mark. They did not appear to have landed very far away, so Karzai took some men and went to get them, but it took more than three hours of hard walking in the mountains to reach the places where the parachutes had landed. When Karzai and the men found the crates of weapons and ammo, they realized the boxes were too heavy for them to carry back. By this time day was breaking, so some of the men went off in search of pack animals, and they found some camels and managed to talk the animals' owner into loaning them for a day. The weapons arrived on camelback the next day at Karzai's encampment, where he group's numbers had now increased to

150 men. Word had spread from village to village, and men had come from various parts of the province to join Karzai. The weapons included rifles and RPG-7s, and lots of ammunition. "And they had arrived just in time," said Karzai, "because by then the Taliban had also found out where we were and the next night they attacked us."

A village mullah on the other side of the mountain had risen at around three in the morning to prepare for prayers when he saw something moving and rushed to warn Karzai. Just before morning prayer Karzai heard the first shots fired, signaling the beginning of the attack. He had a satellite phone, but his men, who had split into several smaller groups at the mountain encampment, had no radios or any means of communicating with one another, so none of the little groups knew what was happening to the others. The firefight lasted for hours, until at about four in the afternoon. Karzai told the tribal chiefs who were with him, "Let's declare ourselves. Let's call a loya jirga. Then, if we die, the call will survive." The call for a loya jirga, in this case, would be for the general population to rise up against the Taliban. From there in the mountains, Karzai called the BBC on the satellite phone.

At first the man at the BBC refused to talk with Karzai. "He said if he broadcast this call we there in the mountains would be killed," said Karzai. "I said, 'Don't you hear the gunfire? Can't you hear the bullets? It's already too late to worry about that. We want to make this call. Please don't kill this moment for Afghanistan.'" The man finally agreed, and Karzai put his spokesman on the phone. (Why he delegated this important moment to a spokesman, he didn't say.) The man said into the satellite phone, "I am speaking for Karzai. We declare a loya jirga against the Taliban. This is a national uprising against them." That was the statement the BBC broadcast into Afghanistan. "And that was the last call we could make," said Karzai. The phone's batteries had run dead.

After the call to the BBC, the tribal chiefs urged Karzai to move his men out of there because they would soon be outnumbered and surrounded, and no one would be able to reach them. "I said, all right, let's go. The elders left first, because they were slower, and they began to move off the mountain. As the rest of us were preparing to leave one of our men who had been on another hilltop came over and said, 'Where are you going? We have won! The Taliban are defeated, they are gone!'"

That group of Taliban may have been defeated, but they didn't admit that to their commanders. They spread the word that they had killed Karzai. By now, no one in the outside world knew where he was, he had no idea what was going on elsewhere in the country, and he could not make any more calls on the satellite phone. "But it turned out that the Taliban's attack on us and their claim that they had killed me was their biggest mistake," he said, "because it caused the people of Tirin Kot to mobilize and take their capital back."

After the defeat of the Taliban force that had attacked Karzai's group in the mountains, the men could have remained there to rest up and plan their next move, but the old tribal chiefs had already gone down the valley. Knowing that the old men were exhausted—everyone was—and it would have been impossible for them to make the return walk up that difficult mountain trail, Karzai ordered his men to follow the chiefs down. The most momentous part of this long journey on foot was yet to come.

7

The Fall of the Taliban

A New Beginning for Afghanistan

K ARZAI'S LITTLE ARMY split up into three groups and left the place in the mountains where they had fought off the Taliban attack, then descended down the valley they had climbed to reach the airdrop site. Karzai's group, eleven men in all, walked all night, heading for a district called Charchinow, where a longtime friend of his had a house. "We walked and walked, hour after hour, in miserable conditions—it was very cold—but through magnificent surroundings," Karzai said. At one point the group came upon a natural tunnel that took them down into a valley, and they found a place where pure spring water was trickling from the hillside. They stopped to drink the water and take a brief rest, and while they rested Karzai checked the satellite telephone batteries. Each one had only a tiny bit of life, maybe enough for one brief call. They would not be able to use the phone except in an extreme emergency. "We were completely out of touch with the world. No one knew where we were or even if we were still alive."

The American and British bombing campaign in Afghanistan had begun on October 7, as Karzai had been made aware of by the pyrotechnics in Kandahar. American and British commandoes and a few CIA agents had also arrived on the ground in several places in Afghanistan to organize local resistance and to coordinate the Northern Alliance's advance on Kabul and Mazar-i-Sharif. While Karzai was in the mountains, heavy fighting had been going on in the north. Now, in mid-November, the Taliban were in full flight and the anti-Taliban forces were in control of half the country. Outside of Afghanistan plans were being made to convene a special conference under the auspices of the United Nations and its special representative, Lakhdar Brahimi, bringing four factions of the Afghan resistance together in Bonn, Germany. As these events played out, Hamid Karzai was walking through the rugged Afghan mountains toward his destiny, and the new beginning for Afghanistan was very nearly the end for him.

"We walked on, and came into a long valley surrounded by mountains, and at the far end of the valley we could see a cultivated field," Karzai said. When we arrived there we found a farmer's hut, very small, with a door only about chest high, and a man came out to greet us." The farmer led the men inside, where his children, who numbered six or seven, Karzai thought, brought the men pots of green tea and some bread. "While we were drinking the tea, the farmer went to prepare for us—and I don't understand how people like him, living so far from villages, keep stockpiles of goods—some very good okra and some of the huge Afghan breads that are baked on a hot surface. We ate the okra and the bread, then rested a while, and at around two in the afternoon we began walking again towards Charchinow."

The men came across what appeared to be the tent of a nomad, from which a man emerged and asked where they were going. Karzai had enlisted a skilled mountain guide from the area, "a clever man who thought quickly on his feet." The guide said they were on their way to a wedding, and they moved on. But the stranger walked ahead of them, moving faster alone than they could in a group, and the guide, suspicious of the man, said, "Let's take a detour." So they headed off in another direction, over another mountain, through a dust storm that limited visibility to less than a meter. At around eight in the evening they arrived in the Charchinow district and saw that the riverbed they would have to cross was full of Taliban pickup trucks, with their headlights on, searching for them. The man from the tent had obviously been a Taliban spy. "We were able to walk quietly across the river undetected and slip into a village," said Karzai, "but the man we had come to see was not at home. Thank God! Because if we had stayed there, the Taliban would have taken us that night." The Taliban were searching door-to-door in the villages, hunting for Karzai and his band of fighters. The group walked on, to a house outside of the village where the sister of Karzai's spokesman lived. The man's brother-in-law told Karzai there was no way he could stay there because the Taliban were sure to come. They gave the men some almonds and some pomegranates and urged Karzai to go back into the mountains for his own safety. "Back to the mountains! We were extremely exhausted, to the point where we thought we would die if we had to walk farther," Karzai said, "but what choice did we have? If we stayed in the villages we would be captured and killed." Wearily, the men turned and headed back, toward the same place where they had received the air-drop, but by a different route—and this proved to be a crucial turning point in their struggle.

After walking for four hours, until midnight, Karzai and his men stopped to rest. One man sat down and was asleep in an instant. He began to snore loudly—so loudly that far away a dog began to bark. "We thought that meant there was either a village or a nomad camp out there," said Karzai. Not wanting to be discovered, they set off again, and at around four in the morning, when it was still very dark, the mountain guide suddenly stopped and turned to Karzai. "Hush! Quiet! Everyone sit down!" he whispered. "Why?" Karzai asked. He said, "I see a caravan." The men looked but could see nothing, only the darkness. The guide said, "Wait. You will see it. Lie down!" So the men lay down and waited, and after about fifteen minutes they heard a bell, the kind that is hung around the neck of a camel. "It was a beautiful sound, coming from far off," Karzai said. "We stared into the night in the direction of the sound and eventually made out the shapes of moving shadows a kilometer away." The fighters lay quietly on the ground until the caravan had vanished into the distance and they could no longer hear the bells, and then the guide said it was safe to move again.

They walked until five in the morning and were, by this time, dead tired. They had been walking almost con-tinuously for thirty-five hours. They came again to the hut of the farmer who had given them bread and tea. He again welcomed the men inside and told them to sleep. "By now he suspected that we were not just simple trav-elers or we would not have come back to his hut, but he said nothing," Karzai said. After they had rested for an hour, the farmer gave them tea, bread, almonds, and pomegranates; it was fall, the season for almonds and pomegranates in that region. The farmer advised Karzai to walk to the mountains the way the shepherds go, avoiding the paths. "It is obvious you are trying to avoid someone," he said. So off they went again, stopping in the middle of the day to sleep on some rocks and be warmed by the sun, then got up and walked until the middle of the night to a place where the guide thought they could sleep safely, in a summer sheep meadow where the nomads had built crude sheds for the sheep. The men slept until morning.

"There we were, deep in the mountains, with no food, no water, and no way to contact anyone," said Karzai. Two men went in search of water, hiking three hours each way to bring it to the group. It seemed the mission was going nowhere and had no plan or purpose.

Finally Karzai's friend Hafizullah Khan angrily pulled him aside, away from the others. "What do you want?" he asked. "Do you want to die here in the mountains? Die of hunger, defeated? Or do you want to win?"

"Of course I want to win," Karzai said.

Hafizullah said, "Well, this is no way to win."

Karzai argued with him. "Yes, it's a way to win," he said. "We'll establish contact with villages soon and then we'll know what to do."

"No," Hafizullah said. "You're wrong. The Taliban must have this whole area surrounded. The villagers can't reach us and we can't reach the villagers. Our strength is gone. We have hardly eaten in days. How can we survive?"

Karzai said, "What do you want me to do?"

"Call your friends in the U.S. embassy," he said. "Tell them to come and pick us up."

Karzai said, "You have to be kidding. They would never do that for me. How can they pick us up here in these mountains?"

"Call them and see," he said.

Karzai asked the rest of the group what they thought. They told him that Hafizullah was exactly right, that they had to find some way out. "This is not winning!" they said. The fighters felt they had made a mistake in leaving the base where they defeated the Taliban, and another in splitting up the group. Now they were out of the reach of any friendly villagers, and they didn't know where the Taliban had set up ambushes for them. "We were lucky the other night when we crossed the riverbed," they told Karzai. "So, you have a telephone—find a way out of here!"

Karzai said, "If that's your verdict, I'll try. But I don't think I have enough battery power to make even one call." During the warm part of the day, he had put the batteries out in the sun to see if that would recharge them a little, but it had not helped. Karzai put one battery into the satellite telephone and called his brother long enough to say he was alive. "Thank God!" the brother said. "Why didn't you call us before?" Karzai told him he had been saving the batteries for an emergency, and before he could say anything else, the battery died. The situation looked bleak. If all the batteries were as weak as the first one, there wouldn't be time to tell the Americans anything, much less give them a position. "I started going through all the batteries one by one, looking for a battery with enough power for a minute or two," Karzai said. "Suddenly—think of the luck!—I tested one battery and it was brand-new, fully charged! How had I missed it before?"

Using the fully charged battery, Karzai spoke with the U.S. embassy in Islamabad, with Rome, and with his brother again. He told everyone that he was alive and in the mountains and wanted a lift. The Americans asked the now-familiar question: "Where are you?" Karzai again told them how long he and his men had walked and in which direction, and they told him to make the square of fires again and they would find him.

That evening the men found a level place high in the mountains and made the fires. The next day Karzai called back and told them that this might be his final call, because the last battery was running low. The American contact said, "We saw your fires. We'll be there tomorrow at eight p.m."

The group went back to the meadow and slept in the nomads' sheep sheds, and the next evening they climbed back up the mountain and lit the fires. "We sat with our guns at all four corners, because the Taliban might also see the fires," Karzai said. At five minutes before eight, they suddenly heard the roar of a helicopter. It flew up from below the mountaintop, circled briefly, then flew off. The men couldn't see it, because its lights were off, but they could follow the sound. Then, just as suddenly, another helicopter came and landed where Karzai and his men were waiting, followed quickly by a second. "What a magnificent sight!" said Karzai. Someone emerged from the lead helicopter wearing night-vision goggles and called out, "Mr. Karzai! Is that you?"

The group came running from the four corners where the fires had been lighted and boarded the helicopters, but as they were about to take off Karzai noticed that one man was missing. It was Hafizullah Khan, the man who had been so angry with him and demanded that he call for help. He got out of the helicopter and went looking for him, calling to him, running from fire to fire, and finally found him wrapped tightly in a patou, an Afghan shawl. "What are you doing?" Karzai shouted. "The helicopters are here!" "I thought I heard something," Hafizullah said. "But it was so dusty I had to wrap myself up."

The helicopters flew for two hours and finally landed in a field somewhere in Helmand, where a number of Karzai's supporters were waiting. Now the little army of ragged foot soldiers had five helicopters and well-armed and -equipped U.S. Special Forces soldiers. They stayed there for several days, during which time Karzai was able to recharge his telephone batteries and make some calls. He was also able to contact Haji Badhur, one of the commanders with whom he had lost touch after the battle in the mountains; Badhur apparently was also equipped with a satellite telephone. Karzai told the commandos he wanted to go to the village where Badhur was, but he couldn't give them proper directions. They told Karzai to have Badhur light fires the same way he had in the mountains. The American commander said, "This time we want to go with you and stay with you." By now, thanks to the years of liaison with the United States in Pakistan and elsewhere, Karzai was seen by the Americans as a potential leader in post-Taliban Afghanistan and they wanted to protect him.

The night after the Americans located Badhur's fires, Karzai and his followers flew there to join forces with him. Four of the helicopters landed safely at about ten p.m., but the fifth, with four U.S. Special Forces soldiers aboard, had to land a mile and a half behind the main group because the dust kicked up by the lead helicopters and the wind had given the pilot problems, so he had dropped off the four commandos and left. Karzai asked Haji Badhur what the terrain was like where the chopper had landed, and then he took the American commander and some of his own people and headed for the location in the dark.

"We had to climb a mountain, and I again became very

warm from the climbing and then very cold in the mountain air," said Karzai. "One of the Americans gave me a wool sweater to wear, which helped a bit." Then at around 12:30 a.m., in the distance they saw people moving toward them with torches and lanterns. "We had no way of knowing if they were friendly villagers or Taliban," said Karzai. "When they came close enough to see us, they called out, 'Who are you?'" Karzai didn't know what to say, so he called Haji Badhur on a radio, who told him to say they were friends of his. "I said that, and the men said, 'How do we know you're friends of his?' I said, 'Here, talk to him.' They did, and then they said, 'Well, since you're not Taliban, we have four U.S. soldiers for you.'"

The soldiers were all okay, and the men began to walk back over the mountain to their village encampment, but the terrain was so rough that one of the Americans broke an ankle and had to be half-carried, moving very slowly. At around two in the morning they reached the foot of the mountain, where vehicles were waiting, sent from the village by Haji Badhur. They drove the men the rest of the way.

"By then we were into Ramadan, the Muslim month of daytime fasting and prayer, so I took my predawn meal and went to sleep," said Karzai. When he arose, the Special Forces soldiers were in the village square, playing with the village children, who had all come around to see the Americans. "I was told later that one of the kids had seen a white hat on one of the American soldiers and had said, 'Al-Qaeda! Remove that hat!'" said Karzai. The Taliban and their al-Qaeda allies had taken to wearing white turbans as a symbol of their so-called purity, and the boy associated any type of white headgear with them, so gave the soldier his own hat to wear.

Karzai stayed in Haji Badhur's village for two more days, and while there the group received another weapons shipment from the Americans. During those days, their numbers multiplied as people came from all over to join the ranks of the anti-Taliban force. For the first time, Karzai was receiving villagers in his role as a military commander inside Afghanistan. One of the arrivals was an old man with a young boy and a donkey that was carrying a load of something on its back. When the fifth helicopter had been forced to land a mile and a half away from Haji Badhur's village on the night of Karzai's arrival, the four Special Forces soldiers who had been put on the ground had stashed some important equipment under some bushes and had not been able to find it again in the dark when the villagers came to rescue them. The old man with the donkey said to Karzai, "We found this equipment under a bush and thought it must belong to the Americans. We thought they might need it, so we brought it here."

On Karzai's second day in the village a shepherd was passing through, and when he saw that the place was quite crowded, he asked what was going on. "Karzai is here," he was told. The shepherd said, "Tell Karzai that Tirin Kot has fallen, and the people are looking for him. They have sent messengers out to many places."

When Karzai was told of this he called his group together. The elderly clergymen who had been with him in the mountains and other elders said, "Don't take his word for it. It could be a trick. Send someone to find out." Karzai dispatched a young man on a motorcycle to Tirin Kot, and he came back with the news that the town really had fallen. He said the red, green, and black Afghan national flag, not the Taliban flag, was flying there. He had gone to see the local council of elders that had just established itself and told them he had come from Karzai's side. The council members said, "Where is he?" The young man told them that Karzai was in his village, Warjan.

"The next day we saw a caravan of fifteen or twenty vehicles approaching the village," Karzai said. "It was the council of elders of Tirin Kot, coming to tell me that they had taken the town from the Taliban and that they had sent messengers in all directions looking for me, not knowing that I had been wandering in the mountains just a three-hour drive from them."

Karzai immediately prepared to move operations to Tirin Kot, a journey of six or seven hours over very rough roads. The caravan of aging taxis and pickup trucks arrived at around ten in the evening and Karzai went straight to the governor's house. Tirin Kot was the first place to fall in southwest Afghanistan.

"Many, many people came to see me in Tirin Kot, including Taliban," said Karzai. "We were much better off now, with generators and other equipment supplied by the Americans, and we were in constant communication with the rest of the world. I was suddenly connected again."

During Karzai's second day in Tirin Kot, a Talib came to him and asked for a letter from him so that he could bring his two vehicles and his weapons to Tirin Kot and surrender them.

"Why do you need my letter?" Karzai asked. "Kandahar is in the hands of the Taliban, and Zabul, and all those areas. Why do you need a letter from me?" The man said, "Sir, there is no problem when I'm on the highways. The problem is when I'm passing through villages and the villagers stop us and won't let our vehicles pass." Karzai consulted with his friends and asked them what they thought. "Give him a letter," they said. "Let's see what happens."

Karzai gave the Talib a letter requesting safe conduct, and two days later the man was back with his weapons and vehicles, which he surrendered to Karzai. That was the point when Karzai began to see the extent of his authority, which was purely moral because he had no real military means. But among Afghans, moral authority counts for a lot. More and more people began arriving and asking him for letters, and he kept issuing the letters, and it kept working. "There I was," said Karzai, "sitting in a small three-room house in Tirin Kot, receiving tribal leaders, signing letters that people far and wide accepted as authority."

While Karzai was establishing himself as the post-Taliban authority in southern Afghanistan, the U.S.-led bombing campaign continued against what was left of the Taliban forces. Some fifteen or twenty days before Karzai's arrival in Tirin Kot, U.S. forces in pursuit of the Taliban had mistakenly dropped a bomb in a remote village called Thori, in Oruzgan Province, on a house full of innocent civilians, many of them children. The bombers had been attacking a known Taliban base about a half mile from the village when either a bomb went astray or the pilot went for the wrong target.

The grandfather of the children who died at Thori came to see Karzai in Tirin Kot and brought him dinner, so that Karzai was his guest. According to Karzai something very moving occurred at that dinner. "I introduced the man to the American Special Forces soldiers, and told them that an American bomb had killed this man's family. The man then said a remarkable thing, something that demonstrated very powerfully the Afghan desire for freedom. He told the Americans, 'I lost seven children when that bomb struck. If I lose the rest of my children, I would not mind, provided you liberate Afghanistan.'"

Errant bombs continued to take a heavy toll of civilians in Afghanistan long after the fall of the Taliban as coalition forces continued to do battle with al-Qaeda and a resurgent Taliban, and not all of the survivors were as forgiving as the grandfather from Thori.

On November 27, the United Nations Talks on Afghanistan opened in Bonn, Germany, presided over by UN special representative Lakhdar Brahimi. Four main Afghan factions attended the conference: the Northern Alliance, a Pakistan-based group known as the Peshawar Front, the Iran-backed Cyprus Group, and the Rome Group representing former king Zahir Shah. Karzai was a member of the conference but could not attend because he had no transportation, and what's more, he said, he did not want to go to Bonn because he felt it was more important for him to be in Afghanistan. But the delegates asked him to address them by satellite telephone. "At the time the conference began I was in Tirin Kot, in a mud house, sitting on a piece of parachute or something on the floor of a very small, cold room," said Karzai, "and I had a bad cold as well, but somehow my satellite phone was hooked up to the conference in Bonn and I spoke to the delegates." He spoke in both Dari and Pashto, and said, "We are all Afghans and we must make sure this country succeeds."

Later Karzai was in a meeting with a group of elders from the area when Burhanuddin Rabbani, still the president of the ousted mujahideen government, called from Kabul and said to him, "I would like you to take over. I would like to transfer power to you."

Karzai said, "Well, Mr. President, thank you very much, but right now I don't know what to say." He was exhausted and malnourished, sitting in a mud hut in a small village. "I didn't know what the world was about, I didn't know what was going on." After the call he asked the elders with him, "What do you think?" They said, "What do you mean, what do we think? Of course you have to do it!"

But Karzai still felt that he needed to consult with all the chiefs and elders who were there with him, so the next night he called a meeting. They discussed the matter, and all agreed that he should do it.

The day the Bonn Conference convened, word came of the death of Abdul Haq, one of the leading commanders of the jihad against the Soviets and a powerful opponent of the Taliban. Haq, a Pashtun like Karzai, had been the top commander of the Hezb-i-Islami faction headed by Yunus Khalis. Fearless and clever in battle, he was the Pashtun equivalent of Ahmad Shah Massoud. Like Karzai, he came from a prominent family, and, also like Karzai, spoke fluent English and had met often with foreign leaders, including U.S. president Ronald Reagan, who hailed him as a hero, and British prime minister Margaret Thatcher. He had served as police chief of Kabul for the mujahideen government in 1992, but the spectacle of Afghans fighting Afghans sickened him and he left, to begin a flourishing trading business in Dubai and London. Soon after the Taliban took power, Haq condemned them as Karzai had, and, like Karzai, he paid a steep price for his opposition: his wife and young son were assassinated in Peshawar in 1999, the same year the Taliban killed Karzai's father.

After 9/11, Haq urged the United States not to attack Afghanistan, believing that the Northern Alliance and a Pashtun counterpart could topple the Taliban with little bloodshed by removing a few key Taliban leaders. But on a foray into Afghanistan almost identical to Karzai's expedition, Haq walked into a trap and was captured and executed by the Taliban. The Pakistani intelligence service, the ISI, was blamed by some for his betrayal. Had he survived, his would have been a powerful and respected voice in post-Taliban Afghanistan.

After his address to the Bonn Conference, Karzai began to move toward Kandahar. "We never fought, along the way, because as we moved from district to district the people would have already taken power from the Taliban before our arrival. Then we arrived in a place called Shah Wali Kot, a district north of Kandahar, and events took a different shape. There, God spared me once again."

After Karzai arrived in Shah Wali Kot a mujahid called him to say that the Taliban leadership wanted to come there to surrender to him. A meeting was arranged for the next day at ten in the morning. When Karzai got up that following morning, he was feeling very cold, and decided to walk to the top of a little sandy hill in the village to warm himself in the sun before the Taliban showed up. "It was Ramadan, and when we do not eat during the day, we get cold," he said. During the night, a lot of American assistance had arrived—more soldiers, medicine, food—as the Americans focused on Karzai as the probable leader of a provisional government, pending the outcome of the Bonn Conference.

"That morning everyone seemed to be up there on that little hill, including lots of children, and some of my men. As I was heading up the hill, someone ran up to me and said that a group of elders had arrived and wanted to visit with me. I turned back and joined the elders in the room where I received visitors." Karzai sat with the elders and they began to talk. A few minutes into the conversation "the room just exploded." The door and windows blew out, and Karzai and the elders were all hit by debris and shrapnel. He went outside and saw bodies, the wreckage of vehicles, and terrible damage to the village. A 2,000-pound bomb had been dropped by a high-flying American B-52 precisely on the top of the hill where a number of people had gathered, and where Karzai would have been standing. "Had those people not come to see me, and if I had not been told at that precise moment that they wanted to see me, I would have been in the exact spot

where the bomb fell and I would have been vaporized."
He lost five of his best men in that bombing, and three
American Special Forces commandos and several villagers,
including children, were also killed. Many others were
injured, including nineteen Americans.

It was the morning of December 5, the day the Bonn
Conference completed more than a week of difficult nego-
tiations over the distribution of power in a provisional
Afghan government.

After the explosion a bloodied Karzai was moved
quickly away from the blast site and sheltered among some
large boulders nearby in case another bomb came. As his
aides were cleaning the blood from his head, the call came
on his satellite telephone from Bonn, and the BBC's Lyse
Doucet broke the news that he had been selected as chairman of the Afghan Interim Government.

The Bonn Conference had settled on Karzai after days
of strenuous debate during which one delegation or
another threatened to walk out. Karzai had the support of
the Americans, which may have tipped the balance in his
favor, but by this time the field of potential candidates had
been severely narrowed by the assassinations of Massoud
and Abdul Haq. Karzai was the logical choice, given his
family background, his close ties to the king, and his long
experience with international diplomacy.

"There I was, sitting among boulders outside the village
of Shah Wali Kot, covered with blood, being told that I
was now the leader of the Afghan nation," said Karzai.
Soon after, an official call came from the UN's Lakhdar
Brahimi, confirming what Lyse Doucet had told him.
While he was digesting this news, and his men and the
Americans were cleaning up the dead and wounded from
the accidental bombing, the Taliban arrived to surrender.

"We went to a room in the village school that we had

set aside for the surrender," Karzai said. The Taliban had sent a very senior delegation—the minister of defense, the minister of the interior, Mullah Omar's personal secretary, and some others. They were brought into the schoolroom and told Karzai that they wanted to surrender to him, as the new legitimate authority in Afghanistan.

"I said, 'Thank you. But you must bring a letter of formal surrender.'" They left and returned that afternoon with the letter, and they also brought a prisoner, one of Karzai's close friends, who later became the governor of Oruzgan, and turned him over.

There were no terms—it was an unconditional surrender.

Within three days of the Taliban surrender, Karzai arrived in Kandahar and set up for business in the house that Mullah Omar had occupied, which was now badly damaged by bombing. By that time Mullah Omar had vanished. "Many, many people turned out to greet us when we arrived in Kandahar," Karzai said. "The foreign press came as well, now that they finally had access to me."

Karzai made preparations to go to Kabul, and he decided that the way to enter Kabul was alone, with no military force whatsoever, not even bodyguards. He called for a meeting of the tribal elders and other senior people and told them of his plan. "Some of them argued against it, saying that I should take three or four thousand people with me to enter Kabul in grand style. But the majority agreed with me: go alone. Because every Afghan is an Afghan, they said, and if a Kandahari can protect you, so can a Kabuli or any other Afghan. So my decision was ratified, and it was absolutely the best decision."

Karzai was flown to Kabul aboard a U.S. military plane, along with his brother, an uncle, and a close family friend. "That was it," he said. "Many people were at Bagram Air Base to meet us, and they had brought vehicles for a large entourage, but when we got off the plane they saw that there were only four of us." It was late at night and Kabul was quiet, as Northern Alliance fighters patrolled the dark streets. Karzai was driven to the palace, where in the morning people came from all over the city and deposited plastic flowers at the palace gate to welcome their new leader.

The new leader of Afghanistan found his new home, the Arg Palace, in remarkably good condition, considering the warfare that had raged around it for a decade. Constructed on eighty acres of land in the northeast sector of Kabul in the 1880s, it has been the home of every Afghan ruler since then, save for Hafizullah Amin. Bullet holes pockmarked some of the exterior walls, and the turrets of the massive palace wall had fallen into disrepair and had been used as latrines. But inside the walls the damage had been minimal. The Gulkhana, the president's office building, was intact and functional, as was the mosque, the residence, a second large office building, and the Dilkosha, a grand house that served as the official royal residence and had been unoccupied since King Zahir Shah was ousted in 1933. The Dilkosha is being restored as a guesthouse for visiting dignitaries.

The palace also housed the national treasury, where a fabulous two-thousand-year-old treasure trove known as the Bactrian Hoard had been locked away since shortly after its discovery in 1978. For many years, the treasure, consisting of over twenty thousand objects of gold, ivory, and gems, had been feared lost in the turmoil of war, perhaps melted down by some warlord. Only a few people knew the truth, and when Hamid Karzai became president, the keepers of this great secret decided it was at last safe to reveal the treasure. The items have now been catalogued, and in 2006 a hundred of the most important were put on public display in Paris.

As soon as President Karzai took up residence in the Arg, he held a series of meetings with President Rabbani and others. Then he flew to Rome to seek the blessing of King Zahir Shah. "He gave me a Holy Koran and his blessing," Karzai said. "I returned to Kabul, and the official transfer of power took place."

In April, Karzai returned to Rome, and this time he brought the king back to Afghanistan with him. Zahir Shah's homecoming had been scheduled to take place a month earlier, but in March security forces claimed to have uncovered a plot to kill the king and Karzai, and the event, so eagerly anticipated by Karzai and millions of Afghans, had been postponed. But not all Afghans welcomed the monarch's return, and in January in the eastern Afghan city of Khost thousands of royalist tribesmen had staged a demonstration to protest what they saw as U.S. favoritism toward the antiroyal Northern Alliance, comprised largely of Tajiks and Uzbeks who had long chafed under Pashtun rule.

On April 18, 2002, the king was welcomed home with a joyous but tightly controlled reception at Kabul International Airport. There was no public announcement of his arrival. When an Italian military transport carrying the king finally arrived at the bomb-scarred airport, security was extremely tight and only handpicked tribal elders were allowed near the monarch. Even so, security officials had their hands full as the tribal chiefs pressed in, trying to kiss the king's hand. Zahir Shah, then eighty-seven, looked frail as he walked from the aircraft, supported by Karzai. Instead of traditional Afghan dress, he wore a coat made of soft black leather, while Karzai appeared in his now-famous uniform of karakul cap and long green chappan.

Zahir Shah is today living in the palace where he once ruled, surrounded by family and friends.

A full suite of government ministers had already been

appointed by the Bonn Conference, so there was a functioning government in place. As chairman of the interim government, Karzai said, "I really didn't do anything much different than what I had been doing—meetings, discussions. More public engagements, of course. Through it all my guiding principle has remained the same: work for Afghanistan. Very simple."

Since the fall of the Taliban, many changes have taken place in Afghanistan, but Karzai refuses to take the credit. "It's not because of what I have done," he said. "The changes have been brought about by the Afghan people themselves, because they wanted change and they were finally free to make it."

8

Building a New Afghanistan

T HE BONN AGREEMENT had provided Afghanistan with a temporary governing body, headed
by Hamid Karzai. The agreement also set forth a frame-
work for the nation to establish a permanent government, including a provision calling for the convening,
within six months, of an emergency loya jirga.The task
of the emergency loya jirga was to choose a president to
head a two-year transitional government. A twenty-one-
member independent commission, made up of well-
known academics, administrators, and religious leaders,
was selected to organize the loya jirga. During the months
leading up to the council, caucuses were held all over the
country to elect delegates; those delegates attended
provincial meetings, where each province's delegates to the

loya jirga were elected in open voting. One thousand delegates were selected in this way; five hundred more were selected by the independent commission.

The commission's work proceeded along a rocky path, as its members dealt with hundreds of complaints, most dealing with the equitable representation of all segments of Afghanistan's population. There were also allegations of vote-buying, but the process of selecting delegates to the loya jirga was virtually impossible for the commission to police, and they had to rely on local councils settling local differences. One contentious issue in the run-up to the loya jirga was whether it or the president would select members of the cabinet.

There was also considerable debate over the role of King Zahir Shah. Since his return to Afghanistan in April, support had been growing for him to resume his role as chief of state. Various potential configurations emerged from the debates, including a scenario in which he would be referred to as "Father of the Nation" but have no real governing authority; another scenario would elect the king president and head of state, with a prime minister to carry out the duties of daily governance.

As the date of the loya jirga approached, it became clear that the council membership had been overbooked—2,000 delegates showed up to claim the 1,500 seats. The loya jirga commission delayed the start of the grand council for a day while it decided who would be excluded from the proceedings, ultimately allowing 1,650 delegates to be seated.

The international community rendered a great deal of assistance in organizing and conducting the loya jirga. The German government built a huge semipermanent tent on the campus of Kabul University, where the loya jirga met. United Nations special representative for Afghanistan

Lakhdar Brahimi provided "extremely valuable service," according to Karzai, in helping to organize the event, negotiating with various people and offering advice. "The presence of President Bush's special assistant [later U.S. ambassador to Afghanistan] Zalmay Khalilzad, an Afghan American, was also extremely helpful, as he spoke the language and had the respect of Afghan people," said Karzai.

Khalilzad's presence may have been helpful, but it was also controversial. He had arrived in Afghanistan during the fight to oust the Taliban and had worked closely with the Northern Alliance. He and Karzai were close friends, and Khalilzad gave Karzai support and counsel as Karzai formed his provisional government. Some delegates to the loya jirga saw him as a behind-the-scenes power broker, using America's influence to ensure Karzai's election. Controversy over Khalilzad's role in Afghan internal affairs would continue until he was sent by President Bush to Baghdad in April 2005 to serve as ambassador to Iraq.

On June 10, 2002, the loya jirga formally convened. King Zahir Shah issued a statement to the assembly stating that he would not be a candidate for head of state, and that he supported Hamid Karzai for president. Karzai, as a presidential candidate, did not have a seat at the loya jirga but addressed the council as head of the transitional government.

"I attended the opening session, and met with a number of the delegations, but after that I stayed away," said Karzai. There were a number of candidates for president, including a woman, Masooda Jalal, who later became minister of women's affairs. Former president Rabbani was also a candidate, but on the second day of the assembly he withdrew his candidacy and threw his support to Karzai, saying he did so in the interest of national unity. On June 13, the delegates voted for president, using a secret ballot for the first time in a loya jirga. The United Nations counted the votes and announced that of the 1,555 votes cast, 1,295 were for Hamid Karzai.

"I was now president of the transitional government," Karzai said. "I spoke to the delegates, saying what a proud moment this was for Afghanistan, that after twenty-five years all Afghans are once more gathered under one tent. I spoke of the need for peace, stability, and security. Under that tent I could feel the immense desire of the Afghan people to have the ownership of their country back in the hands of Afghans."

After the election of Karzai, the loya jirga debated the matter of a new constitution. The Bonn Agreement had established a special commission to draft a constitution for Afghanistan, and the loya jirga decreed that a second council be held within eighteen months to ratify a constitution.

The loya jirga met for a week. Tensions ran high inside the big tent and on the streets of Kabul. At times, blocs of unhappy delegates stormed out of the tent, and a large group staged a one-day boycott because they perceived "foreign interference" at work. On the streets of Kabul, troops of the International Security Assistance Force (ISAF) clashed briefly with armed men who had arrived with Ahmad Shah Massoud's brother Wali Massoud, Afghanistan's ambassador to Britain, but for the most part the ISAF troops maintained order in the capital. On what was supposed to be the final day of the loya jirga, British major general John McColl, who had set up the ISAF in Afghanistan, was honored with a medal, and the delegates gave him a standing ovation.

The delegates had not come to agreement on a presidential cabinet, however, and on the final day of the assembly President-elect Karzai told the delegates that they had run out of time and he would have to select his cabinet.

That touched off a firestorm of protest, and Karzai asked the delegates to extend the meeting for two more days. On June 19, Karzai named his cabinet, which included General Muhammad Fahim, the former military chief of Massoud's army, as defense minister and one of three vice presidents. Another of the vice presidents, Haji Abdul Qadir, would be shot to death on a Kabul street less than a month later.

After the emergency loya jirga finally ended, Karzai and his cabinet were faced with the monumental task of virtually creating a new nation from the wreckage of Afghanistan, including standing up a functioning government and uniting the numerous regional and ethnic factions of the country, many of which were still heavily armed.

"After the loya jirga ended, the commanding general of the U.S. coalition came to see me on an urgent basis, to tell me that he was worried about my security," said Karzai. The general said that the Afghans around Karzai were not trained and not qualified to handle threats from terrorism and provide the sophisticated security required by a president, and he offered to provide an American security detail. "I told the general that I would study this and consult with other Afghans to see what they thought about the idea," said Karzai. He was surprised to find that there was overwhelming approval of the proposed protection among the Afghans he spoke with from all over the country. They told Karzai that it would be the best thing to do and that he should accept the offer as soon as possible. Security is not just men, they told him, it is knowledge, training, and equipment. "So I agreed, and the Americans not only did a great job of providing security, they trained Afghans to take over from them. Now I once again have Afghan security, but now they are well-trained and well-equipped."

The American security force around Karzai, which stayed with him for two years while it trained a cadre of Afghan presidential guards, resembled a paramilitary force; indeed, most of its members had served as commandos in the U.S. Army Special Forces or Navy SEALs. Big, strapping Americans wearing sunglasses and carrying large weapons, the security men were highly visible wherever Karzai went, and were always at his side—and in front of and behind him. If Karzai dropped in to a provincial capital to visit the governor, he would travel by helicopter. The landing zone would be secured in advance by the Americans. If local elders and other officials formed a receiving line to greet the president, Karzai would walk down the line flanked by two security guards while a third, automatic weapon at the ready, walked behind the line.

On September 5, 2002, less than three months after he was elected president of the transitional government, Karzai survived an assassination attempt in Kandahar, where he had gone to attend the wedding of his brother. Huge crowds had turned out to greet the native son, in his first visit to Kandahar since his election. As the presidential convoy drove slowly through the crowded streets, a man in an Afghan police uniform fired four shots into Karzai's car. One round whistled past Karzai's head and struck the governor of Kandahar, Gul Agha Sherzai, in the head. His injuries were not fatal. Karzai's American security guards opened fire on the gunman and killed him. He was identified as Abdul Rahman, a suspected Taliban who had joined the Kandahar governor's own security force less than a month before.

Two years later, a would-be assassin fired a rocket at the president's helicopter while he was on a campaign trip in advance of the nationwide presidential elections in October 2004.

But for the present, there was much to be done. "We

got to work right away on the process of preparing for the constitutional loya jirga," said Karzai. The first task was to appoint committees, one to draft a constitution and the other to review the work of the drafters. "After much consultation with many people, I appointed the members of these committees, and for the next year or so they were left pretty much to themselves to do their work." The committee members first sought input from the Afghan public. They took questionnaires to all parts of the country to ask for opinions on what form of government the Afghan people would like. There were several options, including a presidential system, a prime minister/parliament system, and a return to the monarchy. A clear majority said they preferred a presidential system.

Karzai himself was constantly sampling the opinions of Afghans on a range on issues. "Even before I became president of the transitional government I had been meeting with Afghans from all parts of the country, and continued to do so," he said. "And in those early days the number one thing people were asking for was disarmament, disarmament, disarmament." People wanted the weapons collected from the numerous factional militias and local warlords to minimize the danger of the country's erupting in violence again. The Afghans also emphasized the necessity for the rule of law, in absolute terms. After those things, according to what people told Karzai, came education, health care, roads, water, electricity—all the things the developed world takes for granted. The Afghan infrastructure, never very advanced, was now in shambles. Only about 6 percent of the population received electricity, and even today in Kabul the hum of generators is more or less constant. Many villages were inaccessible in winter when snow covered the mountain passes. Health care was almost nonexistent outside the major cities. Hundreds of schools had been destroyed in the fighting. Karzai's high school, Habibia, the biggest and best high school in Afghanistan, stood in ruins. Yet the Afghans knew that unless the weapons were taken out of circulation none of the other benefits of modern society would arrive.

The process of DDR—the Disarmament, Demobilization and Reintegration of the militias—began in February 2003 and was run by the Afghanistan New Beginnings Program, with support from the UN Development Program and the UN Assistance Mission in Afghanistan. Over the next three years the DDR program collected thousands of individual weapons, artillery pieces, machine guns, tanks, and other heavy weapons and put them under the control of the minister of defense. More than 250 militias were demobilized, and over 63,000 former combatants were disarmed. The DDR program also helped the former fighters reintegrate into civilian life through vocational training and job placement, or back into military life in the new Afghan National Army.

"The demobilized officers and soldiers were offered various reintegration options, and nine out of ten chose a civilian option—farming, vocational training, or business," said Karzai. "They were sick of war, sick and tired of bearing arms."

More than half of the $141 million cost of the DDR program was borne by Japan, which gave material support—mainly vehicles—to the mujahideen during their struggle against the U.S.S.R., and in January 2002 hosted an International Conference on Reconstruction Assistance to Afghanistan. Certainly not all of Afghanistan's arms were collected, but the vast majority of heavy weapons— tanks and artillery—were taken out of the hands of militias and warlords and turned over to the new government.

Afghanistan was not only heavily armed, it was one of

the most heavily mined countries on the world, with hundreds of thousands of devices ranging from small antipersonnel mines to powerful antitank mines buried in its rocky soil. Demining efforts have been going on since the defeat of the Taliban, and the mines continue to take a heavy toll, killing or injuring as many as a hundred people each month. Travelers arriving at Kabul International Airport were often unnerved by the sight of heavily padded deminers probing the earth beside the runways and taxiways; the airport has been largely cleared of mines.

Once the DDR process was under way and everyone saw that it was succeeding, priorities shifted and people spoke more of education and health services. "It always made me very happy that in my meetings, people from every village and province wanted schools," Karzai said. "Each province would ask for a university, each village would ask for a school. I saw children going to school in tents, in bombed-out schoolhouses with no roofs. There is a massive desire for education."

India, which had given Hamid Karzai his university education and his fluency in English, provided funds for the reconstruction of Habibia High School. The desire for education that Karzai spoke of was evident there, where so many students turned up for classes that the school had to operate in shifts, even though most classes were held in tents or in heavily damaged classrooms while reconstruction was going on around them.

Another item the village elders would ask Karzai for was maternity care. "I felt that was extremely important, that men were asking for better maternity care for women," he said. "What it showed me was a great desire for a higher standard of living." Later on, the people would request roads and electricity, which are necessary for trade and commerce.

"Today, electricity is the number-one demand," Karzai said, and his reading of the public mind was supported by an inventive broadcaster. A private Kabul radio station initiated a unique twist on listener-participation radio to find out what people were thinking. A telephone number was given over the air. When listeners called, they heard only the beep of an answering machine, with no instructions. Some callers just hung up at first, not knowing what to do, but others left messages, saying what was on their minds. These messages were then broadcast, and more and more people got the idea. Through this very informal and unstructured opinion poll, the managers of the station came to the same conclusion that President Karzai had: the primary complaint of the Afghan people was the lack of electricity.

The desire for electricity was doubtless reinforced by the flood of electrical appliances that hit the bazaars in the wake of the Taliban's departure. The country was now communicating by cell phones, which needed frequent charging, and by e-mail. Young Afghans took to computers avidly, and computer shops and training schools sprang up in towns and villages as well as in Kabul. Afghans were devouring pirated music CDs and watching DVDs of American and Indian films. Pirated copies of American movies hit the shops within days of the films' release in American theaters, some of them made simply by pointing a small video camera at the theater screen. Watching the DVDs was a bit like being in the theater, hearing moviegoers talk, laugh, and cough and occasionally having the screen blocked by a patron getting up from his or her seat to go to the popcorn stand. Afghans also wanted to watch television, available via satellite dishes, which appeared in even the most remote villages.

"Of course we are planning for more electricity," said

Karzai, "but it can't happen fast enough. That's one of the most important things the world can do for us now, help us to build our electricity generation capacity."

In those initial stages of the "new Afghanistan," right after the outside world had returned to the war-scarred nation, Afghans had very high hopes and expectations—perhaps too high. "I myself thought we would rebuild the country in a few short years," said Karzai. "But of course I was wrong, along with many other people—not wrong to hope, but wrong to assume that in such a massive undertaking that things wouldn't go wrong or take longer than expected." But the desire is still there to get things done quickly. Because Afghanistan lost so many years, people are in a hurry to cover the distance to bring themselves even with the rest of the world, especially their neighbors.

As Afghanistan emerged from the dark days of civil war and Taliban rule, progress was rapid at first—the country had nowhere to go but up—and people could measure the pace of progress. With that, expectations changed. People wanted higher salaries so they could buy better clothing and improve their homes. "In the early stages when I attended meetings I could see how poorly people were dressed, and see the hardships they had endured etched into their faces," said Karzai. "Today they are better dressed and their attitudes are much more positive and hopeful. Life in Afghanistan has changed for the better and is continually changing." Karzai said this in 2005. Since then, as the Taliban have become more aggressive, Afghans have become more frustrated with the slow pace of progress at delivering the services and security they had expected.

The constitutional loya jirga convened in January 2003, and it was a tough nut. "There was much argument, a lot of hard bargaining," Karzai said. "But Professor Mojaddedi, who had been elected chairman of the loya jirga, managed it all very well. He had a wonderful way of dealing with the various people and their interests and points of view." There were over five hundred delegates to this loya jirga, and they were divided into subcommittees to debate the various sections of the constitution. Various constitutional models were considered, and eventually the delegates went with the presidential system that the Afghan people had said they favored. The sessions went on for twenty days, and finally the entire document was assembled and brought before a plenary session, where additional changes were made. When no further changes were proposed, Professor Mojaddedi called for a vote. This was an open vote; he asked that all those in favor of accepting the constitution stand up—and almost everyone stood, more than five hundred people. "Only one or two people did not stand in support of the document," said Karzai. "That was remarkable. Afghanistan had a constitution. And it is a very good constitution, unique in this part of the world for its enlightened, pluralistic approach to government."

One feature of the new constitution of which Karzai is especially proud is that it assigns equal status to all Afghan languages, so that children can learn in their own languages in their own parts of the country.

Women are guaranteed 25 percent of the seats in parliament. But in practice, in many parts of the country, it is difficult, if not impossible, for a woman to campaign openly for public office. The result has been a spate of proxy members of parliament, as powerful men—drug lords, warlords, or chiefs—put their wives up for office.

Although women are by law allowed to vote and hold seats in parliament, the constitution has done little to ease the plight of women in Afghanistan, whose traditionally low status sank even further during the long and often desperate years of warfare and Taliban rule. The status of women is changing, but the process is very slow, especially in rural areas. In Kabul, I saw fewer women wearing the burka in public in 2005 than in 2004, and I would often see two or three women, unescorted by a male, visiting the shops in the upscale Shar-e-now district. Groups of teen-age girls could be seen drinking cappuccino in the atrium of the City Center Hotel, chatting and laughing as they were being ogled by groups of boys a few tables away. But that's Kabul. In the countryside, women's rights are virtually nonexistent. Domestic violence is endemic, and forced marriages are common. Young girls barely into puberty are married off to men in their forties and fifties, often in return for cash payments to the girls' impoverished families. Although the phenomenon is little reported, the Afghanistan Independent Human Rights Commission, chaired by Dr. Sima Samar, has investigated hundreds of cases of self-immolation by Afghan women. The commission identified "forced marriages, underage marriages, and multiple marriages" as major causes of these suicide attempts, most of which resulted in death.

Access to mass media in Afghanistan will no doubt speed the advances in women's rights and raise their status, but speed is a relative concept—it will take a generation or two before real progress is made, and then only if the country is secure and stable.

After the constitution was accepted, the government began to prepare for elections. Two would be needed, the first for president and later a separate election for members of parliament. There was a lot of skepticism in the world as to whether Afghanistan would be able to have an open, nationwide election. There was fear that the Taliban or al-Qaeda terrorists would stop people from registering and frighten people away from voting. "My own expectations were much higher, and yet they turned out to be wrong," said Karzai. "I thought that six to seven million Afghans would register, and that level of registration would be a great thing for us, a huge triumph for democracy. But, in a very short span of time, voter registrations were over ten million!" And that was just within Afghanistan's borders. By the time the refugees in Pakistan and Iran and elsewhere had been registered, the number reached twelve million. "The Afghan people were incredibly enthusiastic about the election, and eager to participate in the future of their country," said Karzai.

The presidential election was first scheduled for July 5, but the challenge of preparing for nationwide voting in a country that had never held such a vote proved more difficult than first anticipated. The preparation of the ballots required a good deal of ingenuity in a country where the illiteracy rate was high and voters would have a large number of candidates competing for the office. In the early going, twenty-three candidates put their names up for president, but six quit the race before the election. On the ballot each candidate's name was accompanied by a photograph of the candidate and an icon that was supposed to symbolize him or her. As most candidates ran as independents, the icons were arbitrary, and if a voter could not read the candidate's name or recognize his photograph, he would have to learn which icon to choose. In the months before the election, voter identification cards were given to all registered voters. There were claims that some voters were given multiple cards. To prevent people from voting more than once, they were required to dip their thumbs in ink after they had voted; there were claims that the ink easily washed off.

The July 5 date was moved up to September, and when all was still not ready the election was postponed again, to October 9.

"In the run-up to elections I met with people from all over the country," Karzai said. "Many groups of provincial elders came to the palace in Kabul, and in good weather I would meet with them under the trees in the palace garden and they would tell me everything that was on their minds."

The meetings within the walls of the Arg Palace were in part necessitated by the security situation—it was risky for Karzai to campaign in public, with the threat of assassination ever present. But the palace meetings were also a brilliant political tactic. Several days a week, when Karzai was in residence, groups of twenty or so tribal elders from all parts of the country were brought to Kabul for face-to-face meetings with the president. One by one they cleared the multiple security checks, passed under the tall clock tower into the manicured gardens of the palace, and gathered in the shade of the massive trees near the palace mosque. President Karzai would emerge from the Gulkhana and walk over to greet them and listen to their observations, their praise, their complaints. The elders must have been impressed by the grandeur of the palace, by the fact that they were speaking one-on-one with the president of the nation, and by the notion of being in close proximity to King Zahir Shah himself. They could return to their villages and tell people, "Yes, I met with Karzai and he told me . . ."

"I remember one very large meeting with people from Paktia, a province a little south of Kabul," Karzai said. "One of the leaders, Haji Abdurahman Zadran, said to me, 'We are not voting for you because you are a Pashtun. We are voting for you as an Afghan.' He added, 'I am voting for you also because I know you will help the Hazara people, and if I felt you were not going to be their president as well, I would not vote for you.'"

In another meeting, an Afghan Uzbek man from Mazar-i-Sharif told Karzai, "I have decided to vote for you because I was a refugee like you, in Quetta, Pakistan, and I saw that the house where you worked was a place where all Afghans went and had meetings. There was never a meeting to which I was not invited. So I trust you because of that."

A delegation came to the palace from Pamir, in the far north where travel is very difficult, "and it was the first time in many, many years that those people had been able to go to a government with their problems," said Karzai.

The president found in his conversations with rank-and-file Afghans that the unity of the nation was very important to them. They wanted a government that represented everyone; this was especially true of the non-Pashtuns, who had been ruled by Pashtuns for centuries. But many Pashtuns favored pan-Afghan equality as well. "Early on, an old family friend from Kandahar came to stay with me, an elderly man," Karzai said. "After about fifteen days, he said, 'I would like to go back to Kandahar now.' I said, 'Is there anything we can do for you?' 'No,' he said, 'I came to see you, and I see that you're doing fine. But I do have one request. Afghans have suffered a lot, and of course you should help anyone who needs help. But the Hindus of Afghanistan have suffered more, and I would like you to help them first, in whatever way you can.'"

The presidential elections were held on October 9, 2004. Contrary to the expectations and fears of many, they were a resounding success, with a heavy voter turnout and only scattered incidents of violence engineered by terrorists. The polls opened at either 6:00 or 7:00 a.m. and closed at 4:00 p.m. On election day it was announced that to accommodate as many voters as possible, polls would remain open until 6:00 p.m., but word did not reach some of the polling places in time. Still, it was estimated that more than three-quarters of the registered voters had cast ballots, a remarkable display of enthusiasm for the democratic process.

"Later," said Karzai, "I heard wonderful stories about the election." Some of these stories were reported in the international news media, which had flocked to Afghanistan to cover the election. One man, who gave his age as fifty, had tears streaming down his face as he told the BBC, "It is like a dream. Twenty-five years of displacement and life away from home have broken my back. Today I feel like I am reborn."

Karzai recounted other anecdotes of election day. "In Farah Province an elderly woman arrived at the polling station and said she wanted to cast votes for herself and for her daughter. She was told she could not do that, she could only vote for herself. 'But why?' the woman asked. 'She is my daughter and she asked me to cast her vote.' The officials said, 'No, sorry, you can't do that.' The woman went away. In two or three hours she returned with her daughter, a young woman who had just given birth to a baby, and the daughter cast her own vote."

Another story came from Bamiyan, where a very old woman walked for four hours through the snow to reach the polling place. The officials there asked her why she had put herself through such hardship to vote. Why should her vote matter so much? And she said, "My life is almost over. I am doing this for my children, and for my children's children." At another polling station a bride in full wedding attire stepped out of a vehicle and said, "I swear to God, if I had not voted I would not have been able to go to my wedding with a peaceful mind." A Kabul newspaper journalist stood outside the Mariam High School polling station for twenty minutes and reported seeing many women leaving the polling station weeping tears of joy. A very old, blind woman of eighty years arrived at the Malalai High School polling station at nine o'clock in the morning, assisted by her grandson. She told a reporter, "I did not sleep a wink last night. I woke up my grandson several times, because not being able to see I was worrying about the break of daylight and missing the chance to vote." And taxi driver Abdul Mateen told the BBC, "This is a dream to be cherished." These statements were typical of voters who ignored the threats of violence to participate in the election.

Karzai's most serious challenger was Yunus Qanuni, a leading figure in the Northern Alliance who had held several posts including interior minister in the interim government. Karzai needed to get at least 50 percent of the total vote to avoid a runoff. When the results were announced on November 3, he had been elected the first president of the Islamic Republic of Afghanistan with 55.4 percent of the votes, "votes cast by people in all areas of the country and all ethnic groups," he said. There were some immediate cries of fraud, but these were quieted by the UN's promise to establish an independent commission to look into charges of irregularities (none were discovered that would have altered the outcome).

After the presidential election, preparations began immediately for the parliamentary and provincial council elections, which were held on September 18, 2005. There were 2,707 candidates for the 249-seat *wolesi jirga*, the lower house of parliament, and 3,025 candidates for the provincial councils. "Terrorists did attack some polling stations and tried to intimidate voters," said Karzai, "but the Afghan people—the candidates and their supporters, and the voters—did not engage in a single act of violence that I am aware of."

The journey of Afghanistan—and Hamid Karzai—from 2001 to the present has been eventful and often perilous. Karzai feels there have been moments of great pride for Afghanistan. "I have a sense that everyone helped to achieve those moments—tribal chiefs, jihadi leaders, the clergy," he said. "We have held this country together after so much destruction, because despite the immense hardships, the brutality, the intrigues and conspiracies, there was a deeply rooted nation of history and proud people who loved their country. When the opportunity arrived, the nation emerged, solid."

Cracks in that solidity began to emerge as Afghanistan's reconstruction proceeded at a snail's pace, frustrating the expectations of Karzai and many Afghans. The slow progress was due in part to the fact that Afghanistan had been a shattered, failed state that needed to be rebuilt almost in totality. It was also partly due to the loss of a generation of skilled labor and educated civil servants in the years of warfare. And security remains a problem. The Taliban, reduced to insignificance by the end of 2001, got a reprieve when the United States shifted its focus to Iraq. The resurgent Taliban have destroyed new schools, executed teachers and administrators, and drawn renewed support from a population who feel the Kabul government is unable to protect them. Karzai recognizes the value of the international help Afghanistan has received and continues to receive, and knows that without the involvement and commitment of the rest of the world the country could not begin to make the journey to stability and security. Much has been achieved, but much more remains to be accomplished.

Afghanistan now has an elected government. "We have returned to the community of nations," Karzai said. "Afghans are on the world's invitation lists again, attending conferences, giving speeches. And this is a tremendous source of pride for the Afghan people, to be back in the international community."

Afghan passports are once again being issued, a hugely important thing, signifying that Afghans are no longer stateless people unable to travel. On the dusty side street in Kabul's Shar-e-now district known to every cab driver as Passport Lane, dozens of people line up daily to apply for the precious documents. Many of them can't read or write, so literate entrepreneurs set up shop on the side of the street and for a small fee fill in the passport application forms. Sidewalk photographers with ancient box cameras supply the necessary pictures.

And wherever Karzai travels in the world, he says, "I am happy and proud to see the Afghan flag welcoming me."

One achievement of the Afghan government of which Karzai is quite proud is the way the old currencies were collected and replaced by a new one. When the new interim government was formed, there were various currency notes in use. "We decided to collect all those notes, eighteen trillion of them, and replace them with a new currency. We accomplished this in three months' time," he said. "The old currency was burned to ashes. When the new currency was printed, the first note was given to a man in Kabul. When he held it in his hands, he kissed it, and said, 'This is *my* money.' Meaning the money of the Afghan people." The new currency went out all over the country, by trucks and planes and donkeys and horses and on foot into the mountains. "And not a bit of it was lost," Karzai said. "None!"

Karzai recalled what a farmer said to him on one of his trips. It's the kind of story he delights in, because it reveals to him what he believes is the real true nature of the

Afghan people. "I was way up north in Badakshan, and I stopped at a local shrine," he said. "Next to the shrine was a little hut where a man was selling fruit. Honeydew melons were in season. The man cut open a melon and gave me a piece and I ate it and thanked him. I said to the man, 'Sir, may your shop become as big as Afghanistan.' The man replied, 'No, sir, that's not what I want. We should all pray that all of Afghanistan will be good, and then my shop will be good too.'"

9

Progress, Promise, and Problems

The Road Ahead

A POLL TAKEN in 2005 by ABC News found that despite all the problems remaining to be overcome in Afghanistan, 77 percent of the Afghan people felt that their country was headed in the right direction and 91 percent preferred the current government to the Taliban. Eighty-seven percent felt that the U.S.-led overthrow of the Taliban was good for Afghanistan, and nine out of ten Afghans held an unfavorable opinion of Osama bin Laden. Large majorities felt that living conditions had improved, that there was more freedom of expression, and that security had improved.

That's the good news.

The more sobering news is that in the same year only 6 percent of the population was on the electricity grid, half of all adult Afghans had no education at all, and Afghanistan remained one of the world's poorest countries. Plus, in the past two years there has been an increase in cross-border attacks by Pakistan-based Taliban and al-Qaeda insurgents, suicide bombings in Kabul, record levels of opium poppy production, and government corruption made highly visible by the appearance of garishly decorated mansions built for public officials. And the longer those conditions exist, the less confident the Afghan people become in their government and in the prospect of a brighter future.

These are some of the problems facing President Hamid Karzai. He knows he can't fix them all by himself.

"Since 2001, Afghanistan has made great strides, but we have a long, long way to go before we can call ourselves secure and self-sufficient," he said. "We have many problems to solve, many obstacles to overcome."

One of the major problems is drugs. A five-year joint effort by the U.S. and British governments to eliminate or at least reduce poppy production has been so spectacularly ineffective that heroin production has, by some estimates, actually increased by 2,000 percent since 2001, and Afghanistan now produces an estimated 85 to 90 percent of the world's heroin and opium. CBS's *60 Minutes* reported in 2005 that opium poppy was Afghanistan's largest cash crop and accounted for as much as half of the country's gross domestic product.

President Karzai has made strong statements against poppy cultivation, but the Afghan government simply doesn't have the power or the resources to combat it. The Afghan National Police are nowhere close to having the ability to fight the drug lords—some of whom are now sitting in parliament—and the vast amounts of revenue generated by the sales of drugs permeates the political structure.

"The drug problem criminalizes the economy, corrupts officials, and finances terrorism," Karzai said. "I am absolutely certain that the terrorists who brought down the World Trade Center towers were financed by drug money and other illegal sources of revenue."

Many observers worry that Afghanistan will become a "narco-state," a country in which the power of the drug lords supersedes that of the state—much as Colombia was in the heyday of Pablo Escobar and the Cali cocaine cartel. "This will not happen," said Karzai, "but the problem of drugs is a very serious one and must be, *will be*, overcome by the Afghan people with the help and cooperation of the international community."

Opium poppy has been cultivated in Afghanistan for centuries. Opium always accounted for some fraction of the East-West trade that camel caravans carried through Afghanistan in the days of the Silk Road. In the 1960s and 1970s Afghanistan was a destination for the hippie culture of Europe and the United States because of the easy avail-ability and low cost of opium and its more toxic derivative, heroin. That's the era in which heroin factories began operating in Pakistan's ungovernable Tribal Areas, refining the opium into what had become a high-demand drug in the West. Then as now, the farmers received the smallest slice of the financial pie; producers, smugglers, middlemen, and street dealers took most of the drug dollar. As demand for the drugs continued to grow, poppy became the lead-ing cash crop in Afghanistan, outselling the pomegranates, grapes, and melons the country was justly famous for. War gave the crop even more significance. Some Afghan mujahideen groups were partially financed by drug money.

With the nation's economy in disarray, some Afghan farmers turned their land to poppy cultivation as a matter of survival; many were threatened with ruin or death by drug lords if they did not grow poppy.

"When Afghanistan was invaded by the former Soviet Union in 1979, millions of Afghans fled and took refuge in other countries," Karzai explained. "Those who stayed behind to protect their homes and farms lived under constant threat from the fighting between the mujahideen and the Soviet regime. No Afghan family could go to sleep at night with the assurance that their house would still be standing the next day, that their farm would not be destroyed by bombs or rockets, that they would have bread to eat in the morning, or that they would even be alive to face the day. Afghans had to plan not for tomorrow but for that day, that hour, that minute in which they were living."

The Afghan people were in desperate circumstances, and in times such as those, it was easy for what Karzai calls "outside elements" to take advantage of the situation and promote and support the growing of poppy. Farmers who had for generations grown melons and pomegranates and grapes, and who had raised sheep and cattle, were encouraged by the drug kingpins to destroy their old crops and turn their fields to poppy cultivation. "In many instances these farmers were ordered to do so at gunpoint, but more subtle forms of coercion were used as well. The drug producers would lend farmers large sums of money in advance, and the only way they could repay the debt was by growing poppy." Karzai spoke of a family he knew that lived in the most productive agricultural area of Kandahar Province, and was forced by circumstance and coercion to destroy their pomegranate orchard. "While the rest of the family migrated to Pakistan to seek refuge, one man stayed with the land and grew poppy instead of pome-granates as a matter of sheer survival," he said. "It would take a lot of pain and desperation to destroy a lovely pomegranate orchard that had been in your family for many years, that you have cherished, and whose fruits you have enjoyed and profited from, but that is what that man had to do." Many Afghan farmers suffered in the same way, plowing up their orchards and grapevines and melon fields and planting fields of poppy out of economic neces-sity or fear for their very survival.

Then came the Taliban, and things went from bad to worse. "There were never heroin factories inside Afghan-istan until the time of the Taliban, when the state collapsed and the drug lords knew they could operate safely inside the country," said Karzai. "Before that, the factories were located in neighboring countries."

It's not that the farmers get rich from their poppy crops—others along the supply chain make far greater profits—but the farmers do make more money growing poppy than pomegranates, and that's one reason why Karzai is reluctant to take a scorched-earth policy against poppy cultivation. He feels for the plight of the farmers, saying, "We have to help the farmers move to alternative livelihoods so that they can make an honest living and contribute to the well-being of Afghanistan and the world."

Not only were there twenty-five years of war, but there also have been long years of drought, beginning in the 1990s and continuing into the twenty-first century. This, combined with widespread destruction of ages-old irriga-tion systems during the war years, contributed to the dev-astation of Afghanistan's crops and livestock, giving farmers another reason to grow a reliable cash crop. Millions of sheep and cattle were lost; they either died of starvation and dehydration or were sold cheaply because the herders could no longer feed and water them. "I know of a man, a nomad, who would give his lambs to passersby because the lambs were weak and dying and he could no longer feed them," Karzai said. "He would say to a traveler, 'Take it. If you can feed it, fine, and if you can't, then slaughter it.'"

Demand is the aspect of the drug problem that the West doesn't talk about as much. Much space in the press is given to the supply side—hand-wringing reports of increases in Afghanistan's poppy production that are not balanced by the fact that every gram of heroin produced in Afghanistan or its neighbors is bought and snorted, injected, or smoked by addicted consumers in the West. But Karzai doesn't want to lay blame elsewhere. "We are not going to tell the West that the drug problem exists because your people are buying it," he said. "That's a problem not only for the West but for all countries to deal with. We have a problem with addiction, Iran has a problem—it's not limited to the West, it's a problem for all of humanity. A British youth, an American youth, a boy or girl in an Afghan village, they're all the same, all of the same value, they are all human beings and we must try to save them from this menace." Karzai takes the position that Afghanistan must simply rid itself of drugs because it hurts Afghanistan; because it is against Islam, Afghan culture, and Afghan ethics; and because it is immoral.

"The Afghan people know this very well, and when I spoke out against drugs on the grounds of morality, people responded," he said. "Nangarhar Province, which had been the biggest grower, reduced poppy production enormously. So did Badakshan, Oruzgan, and other provinces." With Afghanistan slowly getting back on its feet and in a period of relative stability, farmers are once again able to bring their melons and grapes and pomegranates to market and get fair prices. "We are making measurable progress in the fight against drugs," said Karzai.

By the end of 2005, the acreage devoted to poppy cultivation had decreased substantially—21 percent by the UN's reckoning and 48 percent by the U.S.'s measure. The tonnage had also decreased, and in 2004 Afghan security forces seized and destroyed more than 18,000 kilograms of opium and 1,400 kilograms of heroin, as well as 88 drug labs. But since then, production has been rising again.

Terrorists and extremists also remain a problem for Afghanistan, one it shares with nations in many parts of the world, and Karzai feels that the Muslim nations must take a very bold stand against extremism, "against those who use the cover of religion to hurt others and who hurt the Muslim societies first of all." Extremism, he said, is the result of "ill-conceived policies and myopic viewpoints, and it becomes political when governments use a distorted, extreme version of religion to advance their political aims." Karzai warns that no one anywhere in the world has "the luxury of looking the other way" when extremism raises its head. "Those who do will soon face the danger themselves," he said. "In whatever form, in the name of whatever religion or society, extremism endangers all of the world and all the world shares the responsibility of dealing with it."

Afghanistan's difficulty in dealing with the problems of drugs, corruption, and terrorism can be attributed in large measure to a shortfall in the support given to the country after the fall of the Taliban. Large dollar amounts of aid were given and more was promised, to be sure, but the nations who came to Afghanistan's rescue in 2001, chief among them the United States, underestimated the magnitude of the task of creating a functioning state. It was not enough to drive out the Taliban and destroy al-Qaeda's training camps. To prevent Afghanistan from again falling into the hands of warlords, fanatics, and terrorists, the Western nations must continue to provide the necessary security so that the new government can function as it should. With proper security, the Afghans can concentrate on building a national road system, a national power grid, and local and regional irrigation systems. With security, schools for both boys and girls can remain open and begin to eliminate the education gap caused by a lost generation of Afghan scholarship. With security, government ministries and the government legal system can begin to function as they should, and power can be taken from the warlords and drug lords and put into the hands of legitimate authority.

But as Afghanistan was being liberated from the grip of the Taliban, and bin Laden and his Arab (and Chechen, according to some reports) fighters retreated to their caves in the Tora Bora mountains east of Jalalabad, the United States seemed to take its eye off the ball. President Bush had put a great deal of swagger into his pronouncement that he wanted bin Laden brought to justice, "dead or alive," but the small U.S. military force chasing bin Laden into the mountains was not given the troops to cut off his escape routes into Pakistan, and the al-Qaeda chief, the world's number-one terrorist, slipped away. Just when al-Qaeda was smashed down and nearly out, the terrorist organization was allowed to get up off the ground, limp from the battlefield, and begin rebuilding itself. By then, the Bush administration was preparing to go to war in Iraq, which, as President Bush was forced to admit during a news conference in 2006, had "nothing" to do with 9/11. That shift in focus drained funding and military forces away from Afghanistan, putting the success of its revival in jeopardy. And in what seemed to be a glaring oversight, President Bush failed to include any funding for Afghanistan in his 2003 budget; the U.S. Congress stepped in to restore the funds.

Former U.S. defense secretary Donald Rumsfeld was dismissive of requests for additional troops in Afghanistan, including at the moment in 2001 when Osama bin Laden and the remnants of al-Qaeda were trapped, demoralized, and all but defeated in their caves in the Tora Bora mountains. The United States was relying on Afghan warlords of dubious allegiance to do the ground fighting while U.S. warplanes kept up a constant bombardment from the skies. But the Pentagon refused to insert a blocking force to cover the escape routes into Pakistan, and bin Laden simply walked over the border, where he was hailed as a folk hero and was able to attract hundreds of new recruits to his terrorist organization.

At the start of the "war on terror" Pakistan's president, Pervez Musharraf, promised full cooperation with the United States to defeat the terrorists. Since then, however, the Pakistani government has made only token efforts to crack down on the Taliban and al Qaeda, despite repeated protests from President Karzai and pressure from the United States. When Pakistan did send military forces into the Tribal Areas, the operation was met with violent protest, forcing Musharraf to sign an agreement with the Islamic extremists promising to keep the Pakistani military out of the region as long as the Islamists lived peacefully. They do live peace-fully—on the Pakistani side of the border. United States and Afghan military commanders say the agreement has led to increased attacks by Taliban and al-Qaeda fighters, who are allowed to cross and recross the border with impunity. A former Taliban spokesman, captured in January 2007 as he crossed into Afghanistan, told Afghan authorities that

Taliban leader Mullah Omar was living openly in Quetta—
the frontier city where Hamid Karzai once lived and worked
and where his father was assassinated by the Taliban in 1999.

Taliban attacks in Afghanistan have steadily escalated,
and the Taliban and al-Qaeda terrorists have increasingly
adopted the tactics used by the insurgents in Iraq—
suicide bombings and "improvised explosive devices,"
roadside bombs, to attack NATO, U.S., and Afghan
security forces.

At the start of 2007, there were approximately twenty-
four thousand U.S. troops in the country, eleven thousand
of them with the NATO multinational force, which numbered thirty-one thousand. Military commanders and
some U.S. politicians pushed the Bush administration for
additional troops in Afghanistan. Senator John Kerry
(D-Mass.), who lost the 2004 presidential election to
Bush, accused the president of a "cut-and-run" policy in
Afghanistan and called on him to add five thousand troops
to the force there. American commanders in Afghanistan
also asked for additional forces. New defense secretary
Robert Gates agreed, after visiting Afghanistan in January
2007, to ask President Bush to increase the U.S. force
there, but at the same time Bush announced his plan for a
"surge" in U.S. troop strength in Iraq. Some of the
troops for the surge would come from Afghanistan, leaving
the country even more vulnerable. Meanwhile, some
NATO nations have failed to meet their commitments to
the multinational security force.

Afghanistan is being abandoned yet again in its hour of
greatest need.

As president, Hamid Karzai has taken much of the
blame for failing to move his country further and faster on
the road to self-sufficient statehood. He's been criticized
for inaction on poppy cultivation, for allowing warlords to

rule fiefdoms across the country, for allowing corruption in the national government. But these ills exist because post-war power in Afghanistan is diffuse and will remain so until the national government and the provincial governments are strong enough to establish and enforce the rule of Afghan law throughout the country, and that will take a generation or more even if Afghanistan is given all the help it needs. Karzai's lack of forceful action on some fronts can be partly attributed to inadequate support from his international partners in the reconstruction effort—his government simply doesn't have the horsepower yet to move forcefully against the causes of the country's major problems—and partly because of the Afghan buzkashi mentality. Like a khan who won't attempt to stage a buzkashi unless he is certain of success, Karzai won't tread on shaky round for fear of failure, which would further diminish his power. He has taken a number of bold steps and succeeded, such as naming his cabinet when the loya jirga was stalled over the issue, and moving powerful regional figures Ismail Khan from Herat and Abdul Rashid Dostum from Mazar-i-Sharif, both to positions in Kabul where their considerable influence can be put to better use to further the goals of the government.

No one has seriously suggested that Karzai is personally corrupt. Nor does he condone corruption. What he does try to do is bring his personal influence and moral author-ity to bear on the cabinet and parliament to reform the government and root out corrupt officials, which is a less spectacular and more long-range approach to the problem.

On his numerous trips abroad, where he is still hailed as a hero, Karzai's message is unvarying: help us, and you help yourselves. Delivering the 2005 commencement address at Boston University, he told the graduates to "question the notion of national interest" and let "morality and the sense of fundamental concern for humanity guide your decisions." He chided the United States and other powerful countries for abandoning Afghanistan to the terrorists in the 1990s and refusing to see the suffering of its people as their responsibility or in their national interest, until the horrors of 9/11 brought them back. He was given two standing ovations by the crowd of some twenty-five thousand at BU's Nickerson Field.

President Karzai believes there is a great future for Afghanistan, but he understands how important international engagement is to that future. More than five years after 9/11, Afghanistan remains one of the poorest nations in the world.

"Look at how far we have come since 2001," Karzai said. "We have built fifteen hundred new schools and repaired three thousand others. Hundreds of miles of road have been built, and if we continue at the present pace we will have built more than thirty-two hundred kilometers [approximately two thousand miles] of road by 2008."

But the country needs nearly eleven thousand miles of new roads, and the Ministry of Education estimates that seven thousand more schools are needed to provide proper educations for all Afghans.

"We must provide electricity nationwide, because without it there will be no investment," said Karzai. "Health must improve. The productivity of our agriculture has to rise, and the world must purchase our produce." Afghans are more than willing to work hard, he said, but the rest of the world must work alongside Afghanistan so that the nation will eventually be able to live on its own means.

As a poor and weak state, Afghanistan also needs the international community to help mediate positive relations with its neighbors. Karzai feels that the country can again serve as a useful transit point as it did for so many centuries—a long-discussed oil pipeline system from Central Asia through Afghanistan and Pakistan to the Indian Ocean would be an example. But at a time when Afghan-Pakistani relations are at a low ebb, and Pakistan-U.S. relations are contentious due to heavy cross-border activity by terrorists and the Taliban, such a project seems remote.

Afghanistan is getting a lot of help. Billions of dollars have been poured into the country for security and reconstruction, the lion's share from the United States, although in 2007 President Bush planned to decrease reconstruction aid to Afghanistan as well as U.S. troop strength. Other Western countries have also contributed significant amounts, as have Japan and China. "Frankly," said Karzai, "I would like to see more help from the Islamic countries, who have been slow to rise to this challenge."

There has been some private-sector investment in Afghanistan. A modern high-rise hotel opened in Kabul in 2005, complete with a shopping mall, a cappuccino bar, and Afghanistan's first escalator, which Kabulis delighted in riding up and down in the hotel atrium. The Aga Khan Foundation built a five star hotel and funded several historic restoration projects. A number of educated Afghans who had gone to Europe, the United States, or Australia during the war years have returned to take government posts or start entrepreneurial ventures, including radio and TV stations, cell phone networks, and construction companies.

One of the successes of Afghanistan's reconstruction is the Kabul Museum, which at one time held treasures from thousands of years of Central and South Asian history. An ancient crossroads of major trading routes, Afghanistan was also invaded by the armies of Genghis Khan, Alexander the Great, and others. Thus not only roads but cultures crossed there, leaving behind an incredibly rich and diverse treasure trove of historical and archaeological artifacts. Roman coins, Indian ivory, Buddhist reliefs, and pre-Islamic statuary were among the treasures housed in the Kabul Museum, but it was heavily damaged during the civil wars and much of its contents went missing and were thought to have been looted. When the Taliban took Kabul, they stopped the looting of the museum but forbade the display of non-Islamic art. They went to work smashing statues and other art that represented living things, including a number of large wooden human and animal figures from ancient Kafiristan, which the Taliban hacked to pieces with axes. The wooden figures, some more than two meters high, represented the ancestors and animist gods of the Kafirs, the "unbelievers," whose mountain domain in northeast Afghanistan was the last piece of the country to be conquered and its inhabitants converted to Islam, in the 1890s, whereupon the province was renamed Nurestan—"land of light." After the defeat of the Taliban, museum staff began to painstakingly reassemble the figures, several of which are again on display. And to the vast relief of all, many of the museum's treasures were found to have been spirited away by the staff in the 1980s and hidden, along with the Bactrian Hoard, in the National Treasury. The Kabul Museum has been reopened, beautifully restored, and its rehabilitation continues.

The National Archives Building has been rehabilitated, and thousands of documents have been added to its collections. A guard force has been raised to protect historic and cultural sites against looting and vandalism, including the niches in Bamiyan's sandstone cliffs where the great Buddhas stood until the Taliban smashed them to rubble in 2001.

Enrollment in Afghanistan's institutions of higher education has increased tenfold since 2001, to more than forty thousand students, 20 percent of them women.

"We are making progress," said Karzai. "We must never turn back."

When the world thinks of Afghanistan today and looks for the reasons why it should commit resources there, said Karzai, "they need look no further than the horrifying images of September 11, 2001. My God! Those magnificent towers in flames! People jumping from eighty or ninety stories!"

The world came *to* Afghanistan to remove the great danger that had emerged *in* Afghanistan because of the incapacitation of the Afghan nation, Karzai said. "Terrorists and other foreign elements had taken over this country and were running it. To the eye it appeared that Afghanistan was being run by Afghans, but the reality was that it was *not* being run by Afghans." Here was a country with an infrastructure that the terrorists could easily use. Afghanistan had airports, planes, technology, machinery, a history of a capable military with a reservoir of knowledge—and the whole state structure fell into the hands of terrorists.

"But the rest of the world ignored Afghanistan," said Karzai, "thinking that whatever was going on there would not reach them, until it reached New York and Washington, D.C. Any nation that might think of leaving Afghanistan now, before it is able to stand on its feet, protect itself, produce its own bread, and fight off the bad guys who will always be trying to return, should revisit those images of 9/11. We cannot afford another Afghanistan like the one that existed then. We cannot ignore the risk. Afghanistan must be rebuilt, for the peace and security of the world and for the well-being of the Afghan people, which in itself is reason enough."

Epilogue

I N EARLY 2007, as the new Democratic majority took control of the United States Congress, the news coming out of Afghanistan was almost uniformly bad. Attacks on coalition forces and Afghan government entities by the resurgent Taliban and al-Qaeda were on the increase, and a 2006 agreement between the Pakistani government and the insurgents, aimed at reducing cross-border activity, had actually led to freer and more frequent crossings. While Pakistan held up its end of the deal, refraining from military interference in the tribal areas along the Afghan-Pakistani border, the insurgents saw it as an opportunity to launch more attacks inside Afghanistan without fear of a Pakistani crackdown.

Whether the government of President Pervez Musharraf acted naively, which is doubtful, or disingenuously, the agreement had the effect of licensing the insurgents to step up their murderous activities inside Afghanistan. Meanwhile, poppy production was setting new records, and drug money was fueling rampant corruption in the Afghan government. Blunders by U.S. and other coalition forces such as misguided bombings or village raids based on faulty intelligence resulted in the deaths of Afghan civilians, further turning Afghan public opinion against the Western governments trying to help the country rebuild. In some ways, the Afghanistan of 2007 resembled the Afghanistan of the 1980s, when mujahideen based in Pakistan were fighting the against the occupation forces of the U.S.S.R. The U.S. and NATO forces had come to be seen by many Afghans as an occupying army, and no such foreign force has ever been welcome on Afghan soil.

Among members of the U.S. Congress there was a growing awareness that the United States was in danger of losing both of the conflicts the Bush administration had plunged the country into in the aftermath of 9/11: Iraq and Afghanistan. Voices began to be raised for more aid to Afghanistan, where the "right war" had once seemed to have been won, or was at least winnable, even as Democrats and some Republicans in congress were calling for a deadline to withdraw U.S. forces from Iraq, where that war seemed less and less winnable. In a December 13, 2006, *New York Times* op-ed column titled "One War We Still Can Win," Anthony Cordesman of the Center for Strategic and International Studies called for increased military and economic aid to Afghanistan by the United States and NATO countries, warning that the West's focus on Kabul "rather than on the quality of governance and on services has left many areas angry and open to hostile influence." On the other hand, journalist Rory Stewart, in a March 3, 2007, column in the *Times*, charged the international community with what amounts to a gross mis-understanding of the Afghans' culture and values, and of trying to imprint Western notions of democracy and civil society on Afghanistan. The vast sums of money poured into antinarcotic and anticorruption efforts, Stewart argued, have "been wasted on Afghans with no interest in our missions," and other Western aid programs "are perceived as a threat to local culture and have bred anger and resentment." Western countries, while they may be pure in their intentions to help Afghanistan, seemed to feel that change could be achieved by the simple application of Western money, know-how, and values. Those who know Afghans better understand that while Afghans appreciate the spirit in which the aid is given, they resent the assumption that if only they would adopt Western values things would be better for them.

We arrive at a conundrum. Western countries don't feel they should support a society where men keep their women under the burka, where poppy cultivation fuels the world's drug problems, where unelected warlords rule, and where religious law trumps secular constitutions. Afghans feel these things are their own business. The reason they grow poppy is not because they believe drugs are good but because it's profitable. There's a very strong demand for heroin, not in Afghanistan—although there are now an estimated one million Afghan drug addicts—but in the Western countries that are telling Afghans not to grow poppy. If the demand for poppy decreased, Afghans would most likely grow less. The cultural and religious aspects of Afghan life that the West finds unacceptable are more complex issues and won't be resolved by market forces. These aspects will (or won't) change over time, and time moves more slowly in Afghanistan than it does in the Western world.

Radical Islam was not a significant factor in Afghan life

until a foreign invader—the Soviet Union—tried to bring about radical change of its own. Until then, Afghanistan was devoutly Muslim but fairly tolerant, as Western visitors in the 1960s and early 1970s will attest. When millions of Afghans fled the country during the Soviet occupation, it was the extremists who screamed the loudest for jihad and whose screams attracted the most support from the countries in the West, notably the United States, whose cold war mentality couldn't resist an opportunity to embarrass the U.S.S.R. on a foreign battlefield without the danger of head-to-head confrontation. The most vocal of the extremists was the vicious and opportunistic Gulbuddin Hekmatyar, and as a result he got the greatest share of American aid, courtesy of the Pakistani spy agency, the ISI, which served as America's proxy paymaster. We can't forget that in that time the United States trained, equipped, and funded the same Islamic extremists it is now trying to defeat.

In the aftermath of September 11, 2001, great opportunities were lost by the Bush administration.

The most obvious lost opportunity was the failure to capture or kill Osama bin Laden, the mastermind of the 9/11 attacks, and the remnants of his al-Qaeda leadership cadre when they were trapped, defeated, demoralized, and all but destroyed in the mountains of eastern Afghanistan. The failure to insert a modest-size blocking force along the Pakistani border allowed bin Laden and his group to escape into Pakistan. The escape itself added to bin Laden's stature as a folk hero, and that in turn helped him to attract recruits and funding to his terrorist organization, allowing him to rebuild al-Qaeda stronger than before. The decision not to send the blocking force, attributed to Defense Secretary Donald Rumsfeld, turned out to be one of the greatest blunders in the "war on terror" waged by the Bush administration. It allowed the most-wanted terrorist in the world to get back into the game.

When the United States launched its attack on the Taliban regime that had harbored bin Laden and al-Qaeda, almost no U.S. ground forces were employed. The rout of the Taliban was accomplished by Afghan forces, chiefly the so-called Northern Alliance, with the help of a handful of American and British intelligence operatives and commandos plus the considerable weight of U.S. air power. All over Afghanistan, from the former Taliban headquarters in Kandahar, west to Herat, north to Kabul, and beyond, there was rejoicing at the fall of the Taliban. There was near unanimity in support of change from the harsh and ignorant rule of the Taliban and their Arab terrorist allies, who were parasites feeding on the body of a failed state.

Hamid Karzai, though he was chosen by a Western-influenced Bonn Conference to lead an interim government, enjoyed widespread support, which became evident in the 2004 national election in which Afghans experienced the heady excitement of voting for their leaders for the first time. Newly opened schools were flooded with eager students, both boys and girls. Optimism was epidemic. But when the Taliban were eradicated, the Western juggernaut of troops and tanks rolled in, followed by government agencies, nongovernment organizations, and private security companies that flooded Afghanistan with "experts" telling the Afghans what they needed to do to become a proper nation. The Western militaries, their zeal to root out insurgents matched by their ignorance and often disrespect of Afghan culture and traditions, became the new bullies on the block. The Afghans began to push back, and the anti-Western insurgents began to regain the traction they had lost in the hearts and minds of the population.

The rebuilding—or building, in many cases—of the shattered Afghan infrastructure stalled almost immediately in a morass of bureaucratic inefficiency and flagrant corruption. Even in Kabul, which experienced an unprecedented building boom and explosive population growth, the government has not been able to provide electricity and other basic services. The capital was awash in money, yet civil servants and teachers were not getting paid. Training of the Afghan National Army and the Afghan National Police lagged, in part because of payrolls vanishing into the pockets of corrupt commanders and lack of new equipment. Hundreds of millions of dollars poured into the country, yet the most visible signs of the country's new wealth were the massive SUVs that clogged Kabul's dusty streets, the garish mansions erected by corrupt government officials, and the fancy restaurants where well-paid Westerners drank imported alcohol and dined on imported food.

Still, progress was made because so many Afghans were desperate for peace and normalcy and were willing to work for progress. Girls were going to school because many Afghans believed that they should, and many teachers and administrators risked their lives to keep their schools open despite the constant threat of attack by extremists; many rural schools have been destroyed and their teachers and headmasters killed by Taliban insurgents. Civil servants toiled in the absence of paychecks. Municipal workers in Kabul labored to deal with the mountains of trash generated by the tsunami of new residents. Traffic police tried, usually in vain, to bring some semblance of order to the chaotic thoroughfares of the capital. Afghan soldiers fought and died in battles with the insurgents. And Hamid Karzai, the glow of his electoral triumph fading, tried to lead a government beset by internal squabbling and corruption.

The rapid defeat of the Taliban in 2001, and the countrywide celebration of their ouster, calls into question the need for the large contingent of coalition forces to preserve the peace in Afghanistan. With coalition air power on their side, the Northern Alliance fighters were able to quickly rout the Taliban. The alliance, comprised largely of ethnic Tajiks and Uzbeks, would obviously not have been welcomed in the Pushtun south. But perhaps, as the late Abdul Haq suggested, a similar alliance of Pushtun warlords could have been assembled in the south, and perhaps such an Afghan regional force would have been more successful in keeping the Taliban at bay than the Western coalition has been. Hamid Karzai was building just such an alliance at the time, and the Taliban were toppling like tenpins until they finally surrendered to Karzai on that fateful day in Tirin Kot. If that informal, solidly Pushtun alliance had been encouraged to coalesce as had the Northern Alliance, perhaps all that the West would have had to supply was air power to preserve the internal security of the country. After all, this is pretty much the way Afghanistan has defended itself in the past—not with a powerful national army but with tribal alliances that dealt effectively with local and regional governance, much as Karzai's father had done in his role as a tribal chief. The overwhelming majority of Afghans hated the Taliban regime, and once the Taliban had been driven out, the Afghans would have kept them out if they had been given the means.

Instead, Afghanistan was once again occupied by foreign troops, and as of early 2007 more troops were on the way. The moment for a "Southern Alliance" was lost in late 2001, perhaps forever. Whether it would have been a workable alternative to the large Western military presence is sheer speculation. But the overall command and control of those western forces is something that can still be negotiated and might make a difference in the way those forces interact with Afghans.

In May 2005, when President Karzai went to the White House to ask for greater control over the foreign forces on his now-sovereign land, President Bush not only rejected the request but did so publicly, humiliating Karzai. Karzai never spoke of this in public, or to me in private, but people close to the Afghan president told me that he was furious. In hindsight, perhaps Karzai should have been both more public and more insistent in his demands; certainly President Bush should have been more publicly supportive. Now President Karzai has to suffer the awkwardness of condemning the fatal mistakes made by NATO and U.S. forces while being powerless to rein them in. If Karzai and his top advisers had more control over those forces, it would surely make a difference. For one thing, Karzai would gain stature in the eyes of Afghans. For another, the tactics employed by U.S. and NATO forces would almost certainly result in less "collateral damage"—civilian casualties—and in more culturally sensitive treatment of Afghans.

There is hope for peace and increased prosperity in Afghanistan, if only because so many Afghans want them. But the Afghanistan of the future can only be shaped by Afghans on their own timetable and in their own way. The more the West tries to impose a blueprint, the harder the Afghans will push back. As has been said, the Afghans are grateful for outside help, but they resent outside interference. The West should give the Afghans shovels but not tell them where to dig; give them bricks and mortar but not tell them what to build. The Afghans are a strong, unique, and fascinating people. They are friendly and extraordinarily hospitable, but only to guests and never to invaders. They are conservative, but they are not extremists. The extremists in their midst are the products of misguided attempts by the United States and other countries to use the Afghans for their own purposes. It is time the rest of the world treated the Afghans with respect. Positive change will come to Afghanistan, but slowly. If we try to impose rapid change, we will not like the result.

Index

Page references in *italics* refer to photos or illustrations.

Abdalis, 26
Afghanistan, 8–9, *9*
  Afghan Interim Government (AIG),
    80, 86, 89, 178–180. *See also*
    mujahideen
  ancient history of, 3–5, 104, *114,*
    115, 180, 221–222
  British rule of, 5–7, 13, 41, 51–52
  constitution, 188, 191, 196–197
  elections, 25, 197–203
  errant bombings in, 174, 177–178,
    228
  infrastructure, 69, *137,* 191,
    194–195, 210, 220
  monarchy system of, 27–28
  presidential system of, 189, 191, 196
  private investment in, 221
  rebuilding of, 191–197, 203–205,
    220–223, 229–234
  terrain of, 69
  tribal culture of, 25–33, 51–52, 62,
    181, 199–200, 211, 233
  2005 opinion poll of, 209
  uniculturalism of, 37–38
  See also education; United States;
    U.S.S.R.; *individual names of lead-*
    ers and organizations
Afghanistan Independent Human
  Rights Commission, 197
Afghanistan New Beginnings Program,
  192

Afghan Media Resource Center, 15–17
Afghan National Liberation Front
  (ANLF), 17, 50, 55–57, 64–65,
  73–74, 78–80, 107
Aga Khan, Prince Sadruddin, 66
Aga Khan Foundation, 221
agriculture, 27, *129, 130, 139,*
  210–215, 220, 228, 229
Akbar Khan, 6
Alexander the Great, 4, 221
al-Qaeda. *See* Qaeda al-
Amanullah, King, 87
Amin, Hafizullah, 7, 46, 47–48, 49,
  180
Arg Palace, 32, *113,* 180, 199
Aryana, 3–4

Bactrian Hoard, 180
Badhur, Haji, 170–172
Bamiyan, 105, *114, 115,* 200, 222
bazaars, *125, 126, 139,* 194–195
BBC, 108–109, 159–160, 201, 202
Bin Laden, Osama, 7, 10, 24, 63, 83,
  91, 209
  attacks on U.S. embassies, 146
  early influence on Taliban, 18–20,
    111, 112
  9/11 attacks and, 147, 148, 150
  U.S. pursuit of, 216–218, 230, 231
  See also Qaeda al-; Taliban
Bird Bazaar, *127*

Bonn Conference, 24, 65, 164,
175–182, 185, 188
Boston University, 16, 219–220
Boy Scouts, Afghan, *118*
Brahimi, Lakhdar, 164, 175, 178, 187
Buddhism, 4, 105, *114, 115,* 200, 222
burka, *121,* 197
Bush, George W., 149–150, 187,
216–218, 221, 230, 233–234
buzkashi, 29–30, *140, 141,* 219

Carter, Jimmy, 47, 57
CBS, 210
Churchill, Winston, 13
Clinton, Bill, 112
clothing, 19, *121,* 181, 195, 197
Communism. *See* U.S.S.R.
constitution, 188, 191, 196–197
Cordesman, Anthony, 228
currency, 204–205
Cyprus Group, 175

Daoud Khan, Mohammed, 6, 35–36,
41–42, 46, 47, 53, 86
Darius the Great, 4
Dashty, Faheem, 146
Disarmament, Demobilization and
Reintegration (DDR), 192
Dixon, John, 17
Doctors without Borders, 56
Dost Muhammad Khan, 5–6
Dostum, Abdul Rashid, 83, 85, 99,
219
Doucet, Lyse, 25, 178
drug trade, 27, 210–215, 228, 229
Dubs, Adolph, 7, 48
Durand, Sir Mortimer, 52
Durrani, Ahmad Shah, 5

education, 35–36, *137,* 191–193, 210,
216, 222–223, 231–232

elections, 25, 197–203
England, 90
British rule of Afghanistan, 5–7, 13,
41, 51–52
invasion by, 23–24, 150–151, 164
entertainment, 34, 35, 52–53, 100,
194–195
Escobar, Pablo, 211

Fahim, Muhammad, 150, 189

Gailani, Pir Syed Ahmad, 62, 65
Gandhi, Mahatma, 39
Gates, Robert, 218
Geneva accords, 77–78, 90
Genghis Khan, 4–5, 27, 221
Germany, 187
Girardet, Edward, 15
Gorbachev, Mikhail, 72–73

Habibia High School, 36, *116, 118,*
132, 193
Hafizullah Khan, 167–170
Haq, Abdul, 68, 105, 150, 176, 178
Haqani, Jalaluddin, 68
Harakat-i-Inqilab-i-Islami Afghanistan,
62, 78–79
Hazaras, 99, 105, *114*
health care, 191, 193–194, 220
Hekmatyar, Gulbuddin, 16, 17, 63,
64, 65, 98, 99, 230
bin Laden and, 80, 83–89, 111
women oppressed by, 53–54
heroin, 210–215, 228, 229
Hezb-i-Islami party, 17, 50–51, 53–54,
63, 74
Hekmatyar's branch, 78–79
Khalis's branch, 63, 65, 78–79
Himachal Pradesh University, 38–41
Hindus, 200
Hoagland, Richard, 17

horses, 29–31

India, 36–41, 38, 52, 193
international aid. *See* England; United
    Nations; United States
International Committee of the Red
    Cross (ICRC), 71
International Security Assistance Force,
    188–189
Iran, 48, 66, 175
Iraq, 203, 216–217, 228
Islam, 4–5, 80, 97
    extremism and, 50–51, 74, 105,
        215–218, 229–230
    jihad, 14, 17–18, 61–64
Ismailis, 66
Ismail Khan, 89, 99, 148–149, 219
Istalif, 33–34, *133, 134, 135*
Ittihad-i-Islami, 63, 65, 78–79

Jalal, Masooda, 187–188
Jamiat-e-Islami, 63, 78–79
Japan, 192
jihad, 14, 17–18, 61–64
journalists, 15–17, 64–65, 108–109

Kabul, 7, 26–27, 36, 38, 86, 87, 150
    bazaars, *125, 126, 127, 139*
    construction in, *136,* 232
    infrastructure, *137*
    Kabul Museum, 221–222
    Karzai's return to, 179–180
    vendors, *119, 120, 121, 122, 134*
    war destruction in, *124, 128*
Kalakani, Habibullah, 6
Kandahar Province, 70–71, 151–153,
    173
Karmal, Babrak, 7, 47–48, 49, 81
Karzai, Hamid, 16–20, 46–50
    Bonn appointment, 24, 175–176
    childhood of, 31–36

criticism of, 218–219
on drug trade, 210–215
family life, 25–26
loya jirga election of, 185–190
post-9/11 return of, 149–160,
    163–173
Taliban opposed by, 101–112
threats against, 82–83, 109–110,
    155–156, 189–191
university years of, 37–41
in U.S., 219–220
Kerry, John, 218
Khalili, Masood, 146
Khalilzad, Zalmay, 187
Khalis, Mawlawi Yunus, 63, 65, 79,
    176
khans, 28–30
Khrushchev, Nikita, 53
Khyber Pass, *142*

language, 37, 39–41, 196
Laumonier, Laurance, 56
Lorch, Donatella, 15
loya jirga, 10, 37–38, 107–109,
    159–160, 185–191, 196–197

madrassas, 97
Mahanyar Khan, 37
Majrooh, Sayeed, 15–16
Malalai, 6
Malang, Shinkalai, 82
Massoud, Ahmad Shah, 7, 56, 68, 83,
    85, 86, 87, 99, 103
    assassination of, 63, 145–147, 176,
        178, 188
    Hekmatyar and, 64, 88, 89
    Taliban opposed by, 107
Massoud, Wali, 188
Mateen, Abdul, 202
mattress fluffer, *131*
McColl, John, 188–189

Médecins San Frontières, 56
Mohammadi, Mohammad Nabi, 62, 65
Mohammed, Khalid Sheikh, 63
Mojaddedi, Sibghatullah
  ANLF, 17, 50, 53, 62, 65, 78, 101, 102, 111
  as loya jirga chairman, 196
  as president, 80, 86, 88, 89
Muhammad, Mullah Yar, 102
mujahideen, 7
  defined, 47
  drug trade and, 211–212
  Soviet invasion and, 54–57, 77–78, 81–82
  tactics, 68–74
  Taliban roots and, 97–99
Musharraf, Pervez, 51, 150, 217, 227
Muslim Brotherhood, 63

Najibullah, Muhammad, 7, 78, 80–84, 87–88, 99
National Archives, 222
National Islamic Front of Afghanistan, 62, 78–79
NATO, 62, 218, 234
Natou, 34
"negative symmetry," 78, 90
"night letters," 110
9/11 terrorist attacks, 147–148, 211, 223
  Iraq War and, 216–218
  Karzai's return to Afghanistan following, 149–160, 163–173
  Massoud assassination and, 145–147
Northern Alliance, 24, 99, 164, 181, 231, 233
  Bonn Conference representation, 175
  Massoud assassination and, 145–147

presidential candidate of, 202
U.S. invasion of Afghanistan and, 150–152
See also Massoud, Ahmad Shah
Noruz, General, 86, 87

Omar, Mullah Mohammed, 103, 106, 109, 146, 151, 155–156, 179, 218

Pakistan, 6, 13–16, 34–35, 41–42, 47
  Afghan refugees in, 48, 51–53, 81–82
  bin Laden and, 150, 216–218
  border security and terrorism, 227–228
  Inter-Services Intelligence Agency (ISI), 83, 176, 230
  role in Soviet withdrawal from Afghanistan, 48–49, 77–78
parliament, 202
Pashtuns, 31–32, 37, 51–52, 62, 181, 200, 233
passports, 142, 204
Peshawar, Pakistan, 51–57, 67, 91, 175
Popolzai, 26
poppy production, 210–215, 228, 229
prisoners, of mujahideen, 71–72
Pul-i-Charkhi prison, 15, 36, 45–46, 46, 49

Qadir, Haji Abdul, 189
Qaeda al-, 7–10, 23–24, 91, 111–112, 171, 227–234. See also bin Laden, Osama; Taliban
Qanuni, Yunus, 202
Quetta, Pakistan, 51–57, 67, 111

Rabbani, Burhanuddin, 7, 65, 175, 181, 188
  as AIG foreign minister, 80

as AIG president, 62–63, 88, 89, 92, 93, 99
allied with Khalis, 79
Taliban opposed by, 107
Rabbani, Mullah, 103, 106
Reagan, Ronald, 14–15, 62, 176
Rome Group, 175
Rumsfeld, Donald, 217, 230–231

Samar, Sima, 197
Saudi Arabia, 63, 80, 97–98
Sayyaf, Abdul Rasul, 63, 65, 80, 91, 92, 111
self-immolation, 197
Shah, Abdur Rahman, 52
Sherzai, Gul Agha, 190
Shiites, 80
shrines, 138
Soviet Union. See U.S.S.R.
Stewart, Rory, 228–229
suicide, 197
Sunnis, 80, 97

Tajiks, 99
Taliban
  Bamiyan destruction by, 105, 114, 115, 200, 222
  drug trade and, 213–215
  early acceptance of, 97–101
  examples of brutality, 23, 100–101, 104–105
  formation of, 7–10, 18–20
  Haq assassination, 176
  Karzai pursued by, 155–160, 163–173
  Karzai's father assassinated by, 26, 105–106, 109–110
  Karzai's return to Afghanistan and, 149–160, 163–173
  Massoud assassination, 145–147

9/11 terrorist attacks, 145–160, 163–173, 211, 216–218, 223
  al-Qaeda influence on, 111–112. See also bin Laden, Osama
  in Quetta and Peshawar, 52–57
  resurgence of, 195, 203, 205, 215–218, 227–234
  surrender of, 173–174, 178–180, 233
Taraki, Nur Muhammad, 7, 46, 47–48, 49
Thatcher, Margaret, 176
Tirin Kot, 84, 153–160, 172–176, 233
travel, 34–35, 122, 204
Turkmen, 99

United Islamic Front for the Salvation of Afghanistan, 146
United Nations, 90, 105, 106, 202
  Bonn Conference, 24, 65, 164, 175–182, 185, 188
  DDR program, 192
  World Food Program, 67
United States, 187, 233–234
  African embassies bombed by bin Laden, 146
  aid reduction by, 215–218, 221–223
  errant bombings by, 174, 177–178, 228
  invasion of Afghanistan by, 164–173
  invasions by, 23–24, 112, 149–150, 230–231
  Iraq War and, 203, 216–217, 228
  Karzai rescued by, 154–160, 167–170
  security provided for Karzai by, 189–191
  Soviet withdrawal and, 14–15, 47, 57, 62, 77–80, 83, 90–92, 176
  Taliban supported by, 111

U.S.S.R., 1–7, 13–18, 212, 228–229
  fall of Communism, 85
  jihad against, 66–74, 77–82
  1973 coup, 35–36
  1978 coup, 41–42
  1979–1989 war and, 47–57, 61–66
  withdrawal from Afghanistan, 77–78,
    83, 90–92
Uzbeks, 99, 200

vendors, *119, 120, 121, 122, 129,* 131,
  134, 135, 138, 139, 142

Wahabism, 97–98
Wardak, Rahim, 68
warlords, 80, 98, 191, 217
weapons, 64–65, 157–158, 171–172
  disarmament, 191–193
  mines, 193

RPG-7s, 68–69
Stinger missiles, 72
Wilson, Charlie, 14
wolesi jirga, 202–203
women, 7, 53–54, 100, 193–194
  clothing, *121,* 197
  education of, 222–223, 232
  in government, 187–188, 196–197

Zadran, Haji Abdurahman, 199–200
Zahir Shah, King, 6, 26, 27, 35, 47,
  52, 108, 150
  Afghanistan return, 181, 186, 187,
    199
  Bonn representation, 175
  ouster of, 6–7, 180
  on U.S., 79–80
Zia ul-Haq, Muhammad, 57, 62